THE BLUEPRINT ON BECOMING ONE

A Hebraic Perspective for the Bride of Messiah
in a Culturally Independent Church

SHOSHANA RHODES

Foreword by Clay Nash

The Blueprint on Becoming One: A Hebraic Perspective for the Bride of Messiah in a Culturally Independent Church

Scriptures marked as (AMP) are taken from the Amplified Bible, copyright © 1987, 2015. La Habra, CA: The Lockman Foundation.

Scriptures marked as (BSB) are taken from the Berean Standard Bible, Copyright © 2021 Berean Standard Bible. All rights reserved. Available on the Public Domain through BibleHub.com

Scripture quotations marked (CJB) are taken from the Complete Jewish Bible, copyright © 1998, 2016 by David H. Stern. Published by Hendrickson Publishers Marketing. Distributed by Messianic Jewish Publishers and Resources. All rights reserved. Used by permission.

Scripture quotations marked (NASB) are taken from the New American Standard Bible®, Copyright © 1960, 1962, 1963, 1968, 1971, 1972, 1973, 1975, 1977, 1995 by The Lockman Foundation. Used by permission.

Scripture quotations marked (NLT) are taken from the Holy Bible, New Living Translation, copyright © 1996, 2004, 2015 by Tyndale House Foundation. Used by permission of Tyndale House Publishers, Inc., Carol Stream, Illinois 60188. All rights reserved.

Scripture quotations marked (TPT) are from The Passion Translation®. Copyright © 2017, 2018, 2020 by Passion & Fire Ministries, Inc.

This book is designed to provide accurate and authoritative information with regard to the subject matter covered. This information is given with the understanding that neither the author nor the publishing company is engaged in rendering legal, professional advice. The opinions expressed by the author are not necessarily those of the publishing company.

Published by...Freedom Fellowship Church, Oklahoma City, OK

WHAT OTHERS ARE SAYING

Few voices carry the ability to bridge ancient Hebraic wisdom with the heartbeat of the modern church as beautifully as Shoshana Rhodes. The Blueprint on Becoming One offers both revelation and practical application, bringing clarity to what it truly means to be the Bride of Messiah. This is not just theology—it is a manual for living in the unity Yeshua prayed for in John 17. It belongs in the library of every believer, pastor, and leader who longs to see the church radiant and ready."

-Pastor Ren Schuffman
Freedom Fellowship Church

The Blueprint on Becoming One is more than a book; it is a prophetic trumpet sounding a clear call to the Bride of Messiah in this critical hour. With deep reverence for the Word and a unique Hebraic lens, Shoshana Rhodes delivers a revelatory message that confronts division and awakens a generation to the beauty and necessity of true unity.

Shoshana's clarity in addressing identity, covenant, and purpose within the framework of God's original design carries the weight of heaven. It's a timely word for a fractured Church being summoned back to wholeness, back to echad. If you are hungry to see the Kingdom manifested through healthy, unified, Spirit-led teams, this book is essential.

The Blueprint on Becoming One is a Kingdom resource for those who are ready to grow beyond culture and tradition into the fullness of what it means to be the Bride prepared for her Bridegroom.

— Ryan Johnson, Author, Minister
Host of The Blacksmith Chronicles Podcast

The Blueprint on Becoming One is a powerful call to discover who you are in Christ and where you fit in His Kingdom. Through personal testimony and solid biblical teaching, the author shows how identity, passion, and purpose come together when we surrender fully to the Holy Spirit's leading. This book reminds us that every part of the Body of Christ is vital—from the visible to the unseen. You don't need to fit a traditional mold; you need to find your fit. When each believer embraces their unique role, the Kingdom of God advances with power and unity. If you're seeking clarity in your calling, *The Blueprint on Becoming One* will equip and inspire you to step into your God-designed purpose with boldness, humility, and faith. **This is a must-read for every believer ready to live with purpose and passion.**

Dr. John Veal, Best-selling author
Destroying Demonic Tactics:
8 Supernatural Strategies to Defeat
Satan's Newest Schemes
www.Johnveal.org

Shoshana Rhodes is a gifted teacher with an incredible grasp of the depths of the Hebrew language. In the Blueprint, Shoshana shares her personal history of walking with Yahweh and how He would reveal to her by His word what His design is for us. The two parts paired together keep it relational and practical while having incredible depth.

As she was sharing definitions of certain Hebrew words, I would find myself receiving revelation from the Lord as to certain connections between the spiritual and physical realms, such as how the Lord has covered us under His tallit. As you read this, I pray that her words unlock prophetic insight for you as well and bless your walk with the Lord greatly.

Pastor Justin Heckel –
His Presence Church
Founder of Heckel Ministries

DEDICATION AND ACKNOWLEDGMENTS

This work is dedicated to my first love, my Messiah Yeshua, who, from the foundation of the world, marked me as His very own. He is my everything.

Note that throughout this book, you will see that I use the Hebrew name Yeshua Messiah instead of the English translation Jesus Christ. They are the same. In Judaism, names speak identity, so I am more comfortable using His Hebrew Name. Please feel free to use whichever name you are familiar with!

There are too many people to acknowledge and offer thanksgiving for this work you now hold in your hands to mention each individually, but there are some I do wish to mention by name. I want to thank my ministry school students for spurring me on to deeper revelation. Great questions require great answers, and as I'm fond of saying, "You don't know what you don't know"!

I wish to extend my heartfelt gratitude to my local apostolic leader, Ren Schuffman, who not only recognized what Holy Spirit has placed within me but positioned me to follow my passion. He is far better at living out this book than most.

I also wish to thank profusely Apostles Clay and Susan Nash, apostles with national stature who care deeply for so many of us and cheer us on! I admit that I was alarmed when Clay published his most recent book, "Aligned for Conquest". I told him, "You seriously danced around my new book and stepped on it in a couple of places"!

If you don't read any other books this year, you MUST read Clay's new book! One of us baked the cake while the other placed the icing on it (I'm not sure who did which one!).

This work would be lackluster at best without the most amazing Hebrew scholar on the planet, Chaim BenTorah. His teachings dig out both the ancient languages and the culture, making the scriptures come alive and make sense. You think scripture has contradictions? I challenge you to post ALL your issues for this man to address. You will be amazed, while the rest of us are in for a treat! He can be found online at ChaimBenTorah.com. He's also published several amazing books that you don't want to miss!

CONTENTS

FOREWORD

John 17:22 The glory which You have given Me I have given to them, that they may be one, just as We are one; NASB

As a gifted teacher, Shoshana Rhodes has certainly drafted a clear blueprint from her Jewish roots on becoming one. In her words, penned upon the pages of this current book, Holy Spirit has made clear the Hebraic perspective for the Messiah's Bride.

Most of the Body of Christ speaks of and desires unity. Shoshana clearly identifies that, as great as unity is, it remains only a process to becoming fitly joined together as one. I ask as you read these greatly informative words to allow Holy Spirit to bring total spiritual understanding of His truth, of becoming one.

Susan and I count the years of friendship we have experienced with Shoshana as a great and mighty blessing. We are so excited about the release of this book. The chapter on identity is so valuable in the hour we are in. God's heart is shown clearly, and the blueprints to becoming one are given. Read, devour, apply, and be changed! May God bless you, Shoshana, with many more books. I am honored to call you a friend and a co-laborer.

As I read this manuscript, the word that rose in my spirit and mind was the Greek word prothesis. In my understanding, God will use this book to restore many to His purpose.

Clay Nash, Apostle
Clay Nash Ministries
www.ClayNash.org
Network Ekklesia International

INTRODUCTION

The stage was set, lights just right. The audience sat in eager anticipation, ready for a feast of sight and sound. Soft music played, gradually swelling to a crescendo. The curtain lifted. The lead actor opened his mouth, and poetic words poured forth in a deep, resonant baritone.

Behind the stage, a woman beautifully dressed, trembled. The director tried to encourage her, but her visible fear grew with each word she spoke. "I can't do this! There are too many people watching," she whispered. The director reassured her, "You did great in rehearsal. This is no different." But she shook her head. "Yes, it is! I can't do this!"

Frantically, the director barked orders for the understudy to prepare to step in. "Where's makeup? Who's in charge of costumes?" Stagehands rushed back and forth, scrambling to fix the crisis. Time was running out—the lead actress would be on stage in mere moments.

The understudy, pouting in a corner, wore jeans and a T-shirt. She'd always believed she was the better actress and deserved the lead. She hadn't even bothered to get dressed or show up for makeup. Suddenly, she was yanked from behind and dragged down the hall. She swung wildly, striking the makeup artist, giving her a black eye that fighters would envy. Her torn dress flapped in the chaos. Once she realized what was happening, she apologized profusely—but the damage was done. Both her dress and the makeup artist were out of commission.

The director frantically sent cues to the stage, trying to delay the lead actor. But this actor was strict about following the script. After finishing his lines, he paused, then yelled, "Maggie... Where are you? Get out here NOW!" When Maggie didn't appear, he stormed offstage.

As minutes ticked by, the audience grew restless. What was going on? Suddenly, the lead actor reappeared, reciting his lines as if on rewind from before his abrupt exit. A flustered, disheveled young woman stumbled onto the stage. She struggled through her lines, unprepared and distracted.

What should have been an incredible production—the culmination of hours of practice, leading to a standing ovation—ended with murmurs and the audience quietly filing out. What on earth went wrong?

Dramatic productions showcase teamwork at its finest. When everyone works within their area of expertise, extraordinary things happen—things that no individual could create alone. When each person plays their part with excellence, without coveting another's role, the beauty of the team shines.

The director might be in charge, but if others refuse to follow his lead, he cannot truly direct. As Apostle Clay Nash states, "If you think you are a leader and nobody's following you, you're just out for a walk" (Nash, p. 31).

What happened to the understudy in our story? Romans 12:3 says *"For through the grace given to me I say to everyone among you not to think more highly of himself than he ought to think; but to think so as to have sound judgment, as God has allotted to each a measure of faith"* (NASB). When we are focused on the "god of me" rather than King Yeshua, we fail and fall.

In our story, both the lead actress and the understudy were consumed with self. When we're self-focused, we hinder the team, let others down, and—most importantly—we can miss our moment of divine promotion.

David could have gone around telling everyone he was anointed king by the prophet Samuel. Instead, he returned to tending his sheep. King Saul was positioned to slay Goliath, yet his focus remained on himself, not God. But David's focus was on the Lord: "Who is this uncircumcised Philistine, that he should taunt the armies of the living God?" (1 Sam 17:26b, NASB). David faced Goliath, slew him, and secured his promotion. How was he prepared for such a moment? By faithfully tending sheep, and in that lowly position, defeating a lion and a bear. David had already rehearsed his part—when the moment came, he was ready to step into the lead role.

God has given to each one of us a MEASURE of faith. No one individual is the complete package. We all need each other!

The Apostle Paul goes on to say in Romans 12:4-8 (NASB):

> *For just as we have many members in one body and all the members do not have the same function, so we, who are many, are one body in Christ, and individually members one of another. Since we have gifts that differ according to the grace given to us, each of us is to exercise them accordingly: if prophecy, according to the proportion of his faith; if service, in his serving; or he who teaches, in his teaching; or he who exhorts, in his exhortation; he who gives, with liberality; he who leads, with diligence; he who shows mercy, with cheerfulness.*

We are called to run this race for the Kingdom of God, not only with endurance but together, unified toward one goal, rehearsing our part until we can carry it out with excellence. No one is above another, nor is anyone beneath another. We are equally called, gifted, and mandated to do our part.

"There is neither Jew nor Greek, there is neither slave nor free man, there is neither male nor female; for you are all one in Christ Jesus" (Gal 3:28, NASB).

It's time we quit worshiping the "god of me" (or the god of woe is me), wishing we had someone else's part, tearing down those we disagree with, rehearsing our insecurities, or stubbornly sticking to a rewritten script. How about (novel idea) we flow with Holy Spirit and who HE says we are, doing what He asks us to do.

This book came to be while in preparation for writing the curriculum for our ministry school's team-building class. I went on a search for a book that would express the essence of being a Godly team member. We are all called to be a part of teams throughout our lives, especially in the Kingdom of God. Some will be called to be team leaders. Many of us will function as both.

This search proved to be both time-consuming and expensive! Who knew that trying to find an existing book on being a team player from a Biblical perspective would prove to be so trying! We live in an information overload age. Whatever one desires to know is available at the click of a mouse. A simple entry in the search bar reveals that there are anywhere from 600,000 to a million books published annually in the United States alone! There are more books than one can count on Christian leadership, including how to build teams from a Biblical perspective. There are books written for the corporate world on team building. Finding a Biblically based book viewed through the lens of the team members proved elusive.

What you hold in your hands is at least a partial answer to the search. As I began to research materials for this book, HIS passion for this story pierced my heart. You see, when Yeshua prayed his final prayer before He went to the cross, His prayer was that we would be one (John 17). Over and over, His prayer was for us to be one as He and the Father are one, so that the world would know. What has satan fought tooth and toenail all these centuries? Unity! Oneness! Division is killing us and tarnishing His bride's reputation before a watching world. Do you see His tears? Do you hear Him weeping over the mess we've made?

Be prepared to go deep. Be prepared to shed some tears. Be prepared to be challenged!

The primary reference source for this book is the Bible, God's how-to manual for life. It's not just a book of dos and don'ts for personal living, but it is the go-to for living with each other, doing life together, and building effective teams! This book is designed to build a new level of unity within the church, the Yeshua way, using a uniquely Hebraic perspective. Let's see what HE has to say on living and working together!

ABOVE ALL, THERE IS LOVE

It was 1998, and I was sitting in a Sunday morning church service, listening to the man of God expound on who knows what (I honestly don't remember). Suddenly, Yeshua began speaking to me about love. When Yeshua interrupts your day, your thoughts, your process, you sit up and take notice!

He started by asking me some questions. When Yeshua asks questions, He's not seeking information—He already knows the answers. Instead, He's seeking to reveal truth and impart revelation into us.

"Can you rejoice with those who rejoice? Weep with those who weep?" I thought, "I suppose so," but I quickly recognized the lack of evidence in my own life for this ability. I was the picture of stoicism. Even in the most dire of situations, emotion was hard for me to summon. I could take charge, bring order, and stabilize chaos, but showing empathy? That was a different matter entirely. If I were honest, I struggled to *feel* the necessary emotions.

Romans 12:15 simply states, "Rejoice with those who rejoice, and weep with those who weep." But what does this really mean? The context of this scripture is love:

> Bless those who persecute you; bless and do not curse. Rejoice with those who rejoice, and weep with those who weep. Be of the same mind toward one another; do not be haughty in mind, but associate with the lowly. Do not be wise in your own estimation. Never pay back evil for evil to anyone. Respect what is right in the sight of all men. If possible, so far as it depends on you, be at peace with all men (Romans 12:14-18, NASB).

The Greek word for "rejoice" comes from roots meaning joy and grace. One definition is "favor, kindness, blessing, leaning toward, sharing benefit" (Strong's, G5485). Another is "joy, gladness, and delight" (Strong's, G5479). Webster's 1828 Dictionary defines rejoice as "to experience joy and gladness in a high degree; to be exhilarated with lively and pleasurable sensations; to exult."

The Greek word for "weep" means "to weep for, mourn, lament"—to shed tears aloud, expressing uncontainable grief (Strong's, G2799). Webster's describes it as "to express sorrow, grief, or anguish by outcry or shedding tears."

Admitting this, I had to confess that this level of emotional expression had eluded me. I had felt bad for those going through hard times, and I had smiled and laughed with those celebrating what God had done for them. But truly expressing a high degree of joy or sorrow? That seemed unlikely, maybe even impossible.

Then, the Lord led me to pray a simple prayer: "Teach me how to love." All He needs is our permission. And so, my journey began—a journey that opened up a world I never dreamed of.

Being a team member with other believers in God's Kingdom begins, first and foremost, with the ability to love. If we can't bless, rejoice, and weep with others, then we don't truly understand love. Love is NOT primarily an emotion; it is a commandment (John 13:34). It also manifests as a series of actions on our part (1 Cor 13:4-7). Yet, the outflow of that commandment and the expression of those actions must be rooted in emotion, because love, at its core, involves heartfelt compassion.

A wise pastor (who is now with the Lord) once said that we should never allow emotions to control or manipulate us. Instead, we are given emotions as tools to serve kingdom purposes. Kingdom citizens must learn how to properly express their thoughts and feelings, not for personal gain, but for the good of the team—and ultimately, for the good of the individual. They must know how to navigate the inevitable conflicts that arise within a team, and they must learn how to honor and respect both fellow team members and leadership.

Furthermore, believers need discernment: understanding the difference between vital, often volatile, information and personal opinions. They must develop the ability to share necessary truths with love and to receive feedback in humility. In essence, we are called to prefer one another in love, placing others' needs above our own.

Most believers have heard of the different types of love discussed in the New Testament. There are three Greek words commonly translated as love:

- **Agape**: a selfless, sacrificial, unconditional love.
- **Philia**: brotherly love or friendship.
- **Eros**: romantic love.

"Agape" is used in the New Testament to describe a love that is highest, most selfless, and most sacrificial. It's often associated with God's love for humanity and the love believers are called to have for one another. Unlike "eros" or "philia," which can be based on feelings or emotional bonds, agape is not rooted in emotion. It is an act of the will, marked by a steadfast commitment to the well-being of others (Strong's G26).

This definition from a Greek perspective is interesting, yet, in my opinion, an incomplete picture of love. Rejoicing with those who rejoice, and weeping with those who weep, are emotional expressions of love, of agape love. These emotional manifestations are integral, not separate from, love itself.

Given the definitions in Strong's Concordance and Thayer's Greek Lexicon, we might assume that every time we see "agape" in Scripture, it refers to this self-less love—an unconditional, highest form of love. And, to a large extent, that's correct. But what if there's more? Is God's love toward us purely an act of His will, devoid of emotion? Does God love some people more than others? Does He love one person more deeply than another? Are all these expressions of love truly "agape"—selfless, unconditional, unwavering?

John tells us that God is love (1 John 4:16). This means that love is His identity! Does He then dial up love for one person while dialing down the same love for others? John 3:16 tells us that God so loved (agape) the world. In John 21:20, John describes himself as the disciple that Yeshua loved (agape).

While Greek tends to categorize love into neat, distinct packages, Hebrew and Aramaic do not always make such clear-cut divisions. The Aramaic translation for "love" in John 3:16 is *chav* (similar to the Hebrew *ahav*), which signifies a one-way love, an unconditional love extended toward the unloving, such as the world, without necessarily receiving love in return. In contrast, the Aramaic translation for love in John 21:20 is *racham* (the same in Hebrew), which also conveys a pure, unconditional love—but one that is returned, as in the case of John's love for Yeshua (BenTorah, 2016, p. 37).

Yeshua loved the world with a pure love. He shed His blood for the world so that they might know Him.

Yeshua also loved John with a pure love. You see, God can only love with a pure love because HE IS LOVE. The difference is that John returned that love. John loved Yeshua passionately!

As children of the most high God, we are called...no commanded to love one another unconditionally. 1 Corinthians 13:4-7 gives us the "to-do" list. It tells us we must be patient and kind, not jealous or arrogant. We must not act like idiots, be selfish, or be easily provoked to anger. We must be quick to forgive. We also must rejoice in the truth, bear all things, believe all things, hope all things, and endure all things. If you are like most, in the heat of the relational moment, this list floats out the window of soul-inspired flesh and finally returns days later, after the damage is done.

Some people are good with "to-do" lists. Most need more. If, as believers, we can marry these requisite actions with genuine emotion—combining love's outward expressions with its inner depth—we might just discover the secret to true, pure human love. The kind of love that weeps from the depths of our soul, laughs uncontrollably, and is rooted in a pure, Godly love.

John 13:35 (NASB) says, *"By this all men will know that you are My disciples, if you have love for one another."* I've always found it interesting that Yeshua didn't say the world would know we are His by the healings, the miracles, the great messages, or worship services, but by our love.

One of the areas the devil fights most fiercely is our relationships with one another. He takes great pleasure in sowing seeds of backbiting, gossip, slander, and unforgiveness- anything that breeds division. This is where spiritual warfare can often feel fruitless; rebuking demons day and night seems to have little impact if we neglect love.

In this arena, love is our greatest weapon. We must refuse to return evil for evil—and instead, bless those who oppose us (1 Peter 3:9). Love, in this context, isn't just a feeling or an emotion; it's a divine command and a strategic weapon. When we choose to love, even in the face of hostility, we shift the spiritual atmosphere.

We will never turn the world upside down for Yeshua without pure love. We will never truly operate as one team, unified in purpose, without love. It's the foundation that holds us together and the force that breaks down walls of division. Love is not optional; it's essential. Without it, our efforts are powerless; with it, we're unstoppable.

WHAT LOVE LOOKS LIKE

Love looks like a man's blood pouring down a tree, while those He died for hurl insults and mock Him. It looks like the Son of God, suspended between heaven and earth, gasping for each excruciating breath. It looks like skin and flesh ripped from His body, exposing muscle and bone beneath.

It sounds like the screeching of hell's minions competing with the weeping of heaven's angels. Love is a sacrificial Lamb slaughtered for our sins, so that relationship—restored and renewed—might be possible again. It is the most horrific price ever paid for the deepest love ever lost.

And yet, amidst the agony, Yeshua's words echo: "Father, forgive them; for they do not know what they are doing" (Luke 23:34, NASB).

This is what love looks like: unfathomable, sacrificial, and rooted in forgiveness. It's the love that redefines what it means to give everything, even in the face of unimaginable suffering.

IDENTITY CRISIS

I knew I was destined for something, but what? The scripture says that "many are called" (Matt 22:14), but for what purpose? Doing what? Being who? I knew how to navigate worldly things, but life as a believer in Messiah was an entirely different gig. I was street smart, but church ignorant. Four years of what I not-so-affectionately called "God's Brillo pad treatment" led me not to a comfortable pew, but to a crisis of identity.

I had grown from my original revelation that Yeshua really was the Messiah to "I'm bought and paid for with a precious price. I'm no longer my own" (1 Cor 6:19-20). With this newfound "ah-ha" moment came "Now what". I knew I was fearless and built for adventure, but how does this fit within a comfortable modern church? In the "old days", women were expected to care for children, keep house, maybe take on the duties of the church secretary if so inclined, or perhaps be on the worship team if musically talented—none of these fit.

Children made me feel like a fish out of water, and domestic duties such as cooking and cleaning were boring drudgery. I barely passed typing class and didn't play the keyboard or guitar.

I volunteered to help in the nursery and children's church. It was only once every 5 weeks, so I didn't feel too stuck. I took the 2-3-year-olds one Sunday when their teacher couldn't make it. I thought "Kids like cookies", so I brought chocolate chip cookies. No one told me that a 2-year-old must play with the cookie before eating it. They never asked me to fill in again. I'm still not sure if they managed to get the chocolate out of the walls!

Next, I volunteered to help clean the church. Every...single...week. No one else wanted to do this, so I cleaned bathrooms, dusted, swept, and mopped floors. Every...single...week until I quit and moved out of state.

Something I discovered while cleaning was that I had the entire church all to myself. It turned into a prayer free-for-all! I prayed for my family. I prayed for the church. I prayed for the nation and some other nations. I spent two to three hours each week praying, filling the quiet with heartfelt conversation with God.

Something else I discovered was a burning desire from somewhere deep within to pray daily for at least an hour or two. I walked and I prayed. God began to show me things and tell me things. I felt Him pray through me. I would ask for things in prayer with uncanny accuracy and see them fulfilled. I knew I was hearing from God and praying His heart. I didn't understand why this was happening, nor did I know that this didn't happen for a lot of believers. I did know that I felt alive with purpose!

Back then, I didn't know that being a prophetic intercessor was an actual calling, nor did I know anyone else who felt this way. These things weren't taught in church. All I knew was that this was a passion for me. I no longer felt like a square peg in a round hole.

Something else began to stir within me. I attended a conference in Urbana, Illinois, focused on foreign missions. They spoke passionately about reaching lost people groups around the world, about the urgent need to bring Yeshua into the most dangerous places. Their words ignited a fire in me: "Sign me up!" I thought.

But their response? "You're a single woman with a small child. Go find a husband first." Can you picture the smoke coming out of both my ears?! I shot back, "I don't need a husband! You watch and see!"

Yet, God's plans were different. I dropped my son off at my mom's house and went on my first mission trip. I was hoping to preach and even prepared some messages. But life had other lessons for me that trip. One of the teenage team members had a meltdown, and I was tasked with "keeping a lid on her"—in other words, babysitting.

By this point, I had learned enough not to despise the day of small beginnings (Zechariah 4:10). So I shifted gears, caring for the least of these, and kept the lid on the situation. I also woke up every morning at 4:30 a.m., walking and praying—not because I was forced, but because it was a passion in my heart.

To this day, I believe that the success of that mission trip wasn't just because I submitted to leadership or "did my part," but because everyone did what was asked of them. Most importantly, I was interceding daily, long before I even knew that intercession was a thing.

MISSION CRITICAL: FIND YOUR IDENTITY

Find your passion, you will see your calling, then find your fit, and God will make sure you are positioned at the right time in the right place. Don't let anyone tell you that you must fit into a traditional role! Instead, uncover your passion and embrace your unique fit. God did send me a husband (Yeshua sent them out two by two). We went on to become foreign missionaries and live in-country. I learned to preach through an interpreter. I learned the value of intercession not only to the nations but from within the nations. I learned to unpack God's word at a deeper level and discovered my other passion. Research! Revelation! Teaching!

So, what does identity have to do with functioning as a team member on Team Yeshua?

Plenty! If you don't know who you are, who God designed you to be, and the functionality and gifts He placed within you, how do you know where you fit? What are YOU called to do? What's YOUR part? What does this even look like?

> *For the body does not consist of one part, but of many. If the foot should say, "Because I am not a hand, I do not belong to the body," that would not make it any less a part of the body. And if the ear should say, "Because I am not an eye, I do not belong to the body," that would not make it any less a part of the body. If the whole body were an eye, where would the sense of hearing be? If the whole body were an ear, where would the sense of smell be?*

> *But in fact, God has arranged the members of the body, every one of them, according to His design. If they were all one part, where would the body be? As it is, there are many parts, but one body.*

> *The eye cannot say to the hand, "I do not need you." Nor can the head say to the feet, "I do not need you." On the contrary, the parts of the body that seem to be weaker are indispensable, and the parts we consider less honorable, we treat with greater honor. And our unpresentable parts are treated with special modesty, whereas our presentable parts have no such need.*

But God has composed the body and has given greater honor to the parts that lacked it, so that there should be no division in the body, but that its members should have mutual concern for one another. If one part suffers, every part suffers with it; if one part is honored, every part rejoices with it. (1 Cor 12:14-26, BSB).

We (our local body of believers) operate at a supernatural level. We press in, pray for, and expect to see healings and miracles. We expect to be able to prophesy into others' lives. Not only do we expect these things, but we see them! The gifts of the Spirit, as described in 1 Corinthians 12:7-11, are in operation in our midst.

The problem occurs when, because some operate accurately in a prophetic word or a word of knowledge, they then believe they are the mouth. Sometimes God shows us a vision that shifts where we are into where we are going, so then some believe they are an eye. No one wants to be a big toe or a liver, but these parts are vital to our health! The big toe provides balance and stability. The liver cleanses and detoxifies the body (among other functions). We can't live without a liver, and getting around is difficult without a big toe.

Each part of the body has its purpose. Every role, every gift, is crucial—no matter how small it may seem. Recognizing our place within the body helps us stay humble and connected, understanding that the strength of the whole depends on each part fulfilling its divine purpose.

Let's look at what this scripture says:

There are different gifts, but the same Spirit. There are different ministries, but the same Lord. There are different ways of working, but the same God works all things in all people.

Now to each one the manifestation of the Spirit is given for the common good. To one there is given through the Spirit the message of wisdom, to another the message of knowledge by the same Spirit, to another faith by the same Spirit, to another gifts of healing by that one Spirit, to another the working of miracles, to another prophecy, to another distinguishing between spirits, to another speaking in various tongues, and to still another the interpretation of tongues. All these are the work of one and the same Spirit, who apportions them to each one as He determines. (1 Cor 12:4-11, BSB).

Why are there different gifts, different ministries, different ways of working, and different manifestations? FOR THE COMMON GOOD! The Greek word for "common good" means to bring together for mutual benefit. This is teamwork at its finest! How can you benefit anyone if you don't bring what you carry and put it with what someone else carries?

When EACH member of the body of Messiah finds their passion, finds their fit, and learns how to flow not only in who they are, but how they fit within the team, the

Kingdom of God comes to earth. It is the SAME Holy Spirit working all things in all believers. He knows what needs to happen, when it needs to happen, how it needs to happen, and through whom! He is the Team Leader! Imagine His frustration when we begin to bow to the god of me, try to do someone else's job, refuse to do our job, or work to undermine the team. Remember: He is God and we are not!

What if you don't know your passion or your fit yet? Guess what, I know Someone who does! Ask Holy Spirit to show you who you are. Try some things out. Do not despise the day of small beginnings. *"Whatever you do, do your work heartily, as for the Lord rather than for men"* (Col 3:23, NASB). Use where God places you to reveal your passion. What would have happened if I had refused to clean the church? What if I chose to gripe and complain rather than pray? If you firmly believe you can't find your passion by cleaning toilets, then maybe you aren't ready yet.

David was a warrior. He killed a lion and a bear. David was passionate, but only the sheep were witness to his passion, bravery, and skill. One day, the greatest person in the nation summoned him. This would be akin to being summoned by the President of the nation and Billy Graham rolled into one. David had been faithful where he was placed. Then suddenly, he was anointed to be king! We can't even begin to imagine the swirl of emotions and thoughts this brought. Instead of strutting his stuff (NOW they'll know who I am), he went back to the sheep. He had a passion to fight and a passion to lead. Now he was anointed to do these very things, but he wasn't yet positioned. He was still in training.

BOOT CAMP!

It's important that once you find your passion and your fit, you allow God to train you first so you don't mess everything up! This is not like sitting in a classroom working on a degree. This is boot camp! You have officially joined the Lord's army, and now you must allow God to prove you so you are fit for service.

Suffer hardship with me, as a good soldier of Christ Jesus. No soldier in active service entangles himself in the affairs of everyday life, so that he may please the one who enlisted him as a soldier" (2 Tim 2:3-4, NASB).

Suffer!?! Hardship!?! I thought I would be safe! I thought life would be great! These words were written by arguably one of the greatest men of God on the planet. No one likes boot camp, but it's necessary for survival as we lock horns with the adversary.

David spent many years in the wilderness fleeing the wrath of Saul before he became king. David wrote: *"Blessed be the LORD, my rock, Who trains my hands for war, And my fingers for battle"* (Ps 144:1, NASB). Yeshua Himself stated, *"In the world you will have tribulation. But take courage; I have overcome the world!"* (John 16:33, NASB).

We have a saying these days where we wish others safety. We say things like "safe travel" and "stay safe". What if we aren't supposed to stay "safe"? According to Webster's 1828 dictionary, the definition of "safe" is: *"Free from danger of any kind; Free from hurt, injury or damage; Not exposing to danger. No longer dangerous".* I don't know about you, but I WANT to be dangerous to the kingdom of darkness! How can I storm the gates of hell and lead captivity captive if I'm living in safety?

How about being protected instead? The definition of protect is: *"To cover or shield from danger or injury; to defend; to guard"* (Webster, 1828). This definition implies a position of danger that requires defending and guarding.

As we become trained to flow in our passion, there will be trouble! There will be attacks. We will be slandered, judged, condemned, and misunderstood. Church members encumbered by the chains of tradition will try to place us in ill-fitting positions, not because they desire to train and raise up disciples, but because they have a hole they need to fill. They will attempt to burn us out and condemn us for not sticking to THEIR plan for our lives. It's up to us to recognize if this is our sheep-tending, toilet-cleaning season so we can glean what we need, or if this is where we face off with Goliath.

MOVING FROM THE TRAINING GROUND
TO THE PLACE OF POSITIONING

After returning from the foreign mission field, I finally knew who I was, but I hadn't found my fit. I served in this church and then that one. This was in the post-Brownsville Revival days. God would send me to a church where the pastor was praying for help, praying for true revival like Brownsville. As an intercessor, I would press in. Fasting and prayer became a lifestyle. Dreams and visions became more real. I had read just enough to know that true revival does not come except that there is intercession.

We held church prayer meetings, sometimes just a few, sometimes many would come. The presence of God would fill the room, but it lacked the community out-cry for repentance, the Pentecostal fire, the miracles, the undeniable move of God. Instead, issues would surface within leadership—things hidden, unresolved. There was no true repentance, only sweeping problems under the rug, pretending everything was okay, and returning to church as usual.

God would then give my husband and me our new set of orders, and we would move. I asked God why we had to keep moving. He reminded me that we were bought and paid for with a price, we are in His army, and the saddest part of all, He said that very few were willing to pack up and move on His command. We were willing.

He sent us to several small churches, always with the same outcome. Finally, I told the Lord that I was done with the local church. I felt used, abused, and misunderstood! I became a faithful member of Glory of Zion's online community. Three or four times a year, I would travel to Corinth, TX. The problem? I recognized many of them, but to them, I was a face in a sea of faces. There was no community. There is no fit without being part of a team, and it's impossible to be part of a team online by yourself!

Did you know that God sneaks up on us sometimes? He snuck up on me! I was scrolling through the internet when I found a non-denominational church I hadn't seen before. I told my husband that I was going to check it out. He said to let him know if it was worth his time to go. Long story short, I've been at Freedom Fellowship Church in Oklahoma City longer than any other duty station. It was here that I not only found my fit, but was finally positioned into my calling!

Greatness inspires greatness. David's father and brothers didn't recognize who David was, but God knew and sent the prophet Samuel to pour out God's stamp of approval on his true identity. Dale Mast writes concerning identity, "God will bring new people into our lives to shift our identity with new honor. They will open doors for us that we could not access by ourselves, and they will give us honor among those who have greater honor" (Mast, 2015). David required Samuel to shift his identity.

Joseph also had God-sized dreams. Without knowing the outcome, his brothers ensured his future identity by selling him into slavery! In this life, you will have trouble. Joseph was faithful in his slavery, toilet-cleaning season. THEN he was tossed into prison! He could have been bitter, but he still had God-sized dreams. He honed his dream interpretation skills in prison, which later led him to the palace! His passion was birthed in his father's house, but he was positioned through Pharoah's butler.

Both men, destined for greatness, found their passions in lowly settings, honed their skills in wilderness seasons, and were positioned by someone with influence. We must be faithful in the wilderness, but also keep on the lookout for those who should be positioning us. You will never find your fit without being positioned.

I can't stress this enough: It's important to hear from the Lord regarding your immediate positioning and be faithful to where you are currently placed. Do not despise the day of small beginnings. Remember the lessons of David and Joseph. HOWEVER, when it is time to be positioned, step up! Moses was faithful to tend his father-in-law's sheep for 40 years, but when God called, he went. Joseph was faithful in his placements for 17 years, but when God called through Pharaoh, he went.

The person God uses to position you might not look like what you expect. Listen carefully to His voice, and when He calls, go - regardless of how unlikely the situation may seem. Trust that God's timing and His methods are perfect. Hear from God, and then step out boldly - because your moment of divine positioning is waiting.

IDENTITY: DISCOVERING WHO GOD MADE YOU TO BE

We teach this all the time in our ministry school: Find your passion, and you will find your identity. Many people dismiss their passions, thinking they're not "spiritual enough" or significant enough to matter. When we picture serving the King of the universe, we often envision great preachers like Billy Graham or famous missionaries like Amy Carmichael or John G. Lake. But then, reality hits.

We realize we may never be like those towering giants of faith. The enemy sows seeds of discouragement, and before we know it, we're stuck- stuck in the same rut, same doubts, same limitations we've known all our lives.

But what if we're only seeing the tip of an incredible iceberg? What if this iceberg has the power to blast through the gates of hell and lead captivity captive?

What if there's a hole in that iceberg—shaped just like you—that's causing it to lose momentum? You might not see it because your part is beneath the waterline, hidden from view. But that part, that hole, is crucial. It's the key to unleashing the full power of what God has placed inside you.

Your unique passion, your hidden part, is vital. Don't underestimate what God can do through your "underwater" role. When you embrace it, when you step into your true identity, you become a force that can shake the gates of hell and set captives free.

In 1934, a traveling evangelist named Mordecai Ham set up his revival tent in North Carolina. Mordecai Ham is not a name that many of us are familiar with. He ministered almost a century ago. Two teenage boys attended that particular meeting and asked Yeshua to be their Lord and Savior. One of those boys was Billy Graham. Mordecai Ham played a vital role in the bigger picture. God positioned Billy Graham to win millions of souls for His kingdom.

Billy Graham came to my city in the early 1980s. He was doing a stadium event, and the call was put out for volunteers. Hundreds of us answered that call. We were each assigned a section to monitor, hand out decision cards to those who had gone forward during the altar call, and make sure those cards were placed in a bucket that would be distributed to local churches for follow-up.

That night, Billy Graham's message was simple, yet powerful. The response was overwhelming. I was astounded at the number of people who came forward for salvation. We scrambled to keep up with the flow of those making decisions. To this day, I still meet people whose lives were changed directly because of Billy Graham's evangelism.

Would Billy Graham's ministry have been as effective without the hundreds of volunteers? Probably not. Yes, the same number of people would have responded to the altar call, but then what? Matthew 13:3-9 tells the story of the Sower who sowed the seed of the Word of God. The problem is that some of the seeds fall on rocks, some the birds eat up, and some fall among thorns. Some seeds fall in good ground but bring forth varying amounts. What's the difference? The seed is the same in all instances, but where it lands and how it's nurtured afterward determines its productivity. In the same way, your role—no matter how small it may seem—is crucial. It's part of the process of transforming lives for the kingdom.

Without volunteers collecting everyone's contact information and providing follow-up, the seed that falls among thorns is choked out. There is no one there to spot the weeds and thorns and help remove them. When the seed falls on stony ground, there is no one there to instruct concerning the attack of the enemy, and new believers are lost. Without a church community, no one drives the birds off, thereby protecting the seed.

It's a basic principle: babies are not born and left to fend for themselves. Without daily care—food, clothing, love—they cannot survive. Yet, as believers in Messiah, we often get excited when someone makes a decision for Yeshua. But what about the follow-up? Do we nurture the little ones in faith? Do we teach them how to feed themselves with the Word of God? Do we provide community where they can belong? Are we available to fight off the adversary when he attacks—and he will!—and love them through the hard times?

Acts 2:46-47 (BSB) says, *"With one accord they continued to meet daily in the temple courts and to break bread from house to house, sharing their meals with gladness and sincerity of heart, praising God and enjoying the favor of all the people. And the Lord added to their number daily those who were being saved."* God's people encouraged each other in community, and as a result, He added to their numbers DAILY!

So, how can we be trusted with a daily increase of newborns when we aren't willing to take the time to care for the ones we already have? If we neglect the little ones, how can we expect to see the fullness of God's harvest?

THE BAD OLD DAYS

When I met Yeshua many decades ago, I was simply told to attend church on Sunday and read the Bible. No one taught me about spiritual warfare. No one explained how to navigate the hard times. I was taught all about the "dos and don'ts," but not how to cultivate a deep, personal relationship with a God who could love me through every trial and tribulation.

I encountered Yeshua at the end of the Jesus People movement of the 1970s. I was a stubborn, rebellious hot mess—yet through the grace of God, I survived. Most of my generation did not.

Did I help to save a soul, a precious life, that day in that Billy Graham meeting? I won't know the full impact until I stand before Him. But I believe I did—probably. Did those lives survive "church as usual"? Only God knows.

What I do know is this: Every seed sown, every act of obedience, has eternal significance. We may never see the full harvest in our lifetime, but God is always at work. And in His divine mercy, He takes our efforts—whether we see immediate fruit or not—and weaves them into His greater plan.

What's your part? At that, and many other stadium and ministry events where I've had the privilege of serving, it took an army of people to make everything happen. Some served refreshments, some cleaned and restocked the bathrooms, some provided security, and many local pastors had to agree not only to be on the list but to actually provide the requested follow-up. There were intercessors behind the scenes praying for it all to come together, binding the forces of darkness from interfering, removing veils from participants' eyes. The worship team had to practice so that the atmosphere was properly set. Advertisers had to get the word out about the event. The tech team had to make sure everything was properly set up and running smoothly. You get the picture.

WHAT'S YOUR PART?

You may never preach a message before a group of people in your life, but YOUR part is VITAL. It's NOT for the success of the preacher. It's for the love and service of the King! It's for the least of these. Your part is vital to save the lives of the newborns and nurture them to maturity. Your part is crucial. Whether in small acts of kindness, consistent prayer, or faithful service, you are an essential part of the body, making sure the seed of the Gospel takes root and flourishes. Every act of obedience, every act of love, contributes to the eternal harvest.

Some of you are "Yes! Send me the little ones so I can love on them, care for them, and raise them up!" Some of you are "Noooo! I don't know how to nurture! I feel like a fish out of water!" Go back and read again 1 Cor 12:14-26. If God created you with an aptitude for technology, ministry events fall flat without you. Attendees become distracted by amateur attempts to pull off sight, sound, and video. Instead of Holy Spirit ministering to that one in the audience with a deep revelation, THAT person is sitting there thinking, "This is messed up. I can run sound better than that!" Without the part you are called to play, there's a you-shaped hole in the iceberg. It may look good above the surface, but too many holes below the surface can cause it to be upended.

Some ministries die because those in leadership don't understand the vital importance of community. They try to do everything themselves, hit a wall, and burn out. Some ministries die because those "less seemly members" get jealous of those in the limelight and begin the gossip and backbiting cycle, or worse, lead a church split.

So, how do we know who we are? How do we make sure to fulfill our part of the great commission, so we can save the less fortunate seed from the enemy's birds, thorns, and blistering sun? How do we position ourselves to hear *"Well done, good and faithful servant! You have been faithful with a few things; I will put you in charge of many things. Enter into the joy of your master!"* (Matt 25:21, BSB).

The answer begins with prayer, humility, and an open heart. Ask Holy Spirit to reveal your unique place in His kingdom. Discover your gifts, embrace your calling, and step into the role God has prepared for you. When each of us fulfills our divine purpose, the body functions perfectly, and a great harvest is reaped.

FINDING IDENTITY IN THE SECRET PLACE

What if you don't yet know who you truly are? What if your passion—the thing that makes you come alive—remains hidden? Your identity is fundamentally a reflection of Yeshua. But how can you mirror Him if you haven't spent time with Him?

This isn't just about what you do; it's about cultivating a deep, ongoing relationship with Him. The more time you spend in His presence—praying, worshiping, listening—the more His character is formed within you. Out of that intimate connection, your passions will emerge, and your true identity will unfold.

The secret place is where your identity is forged—where you discover who you are in Him. It's not about striving or trying to find your purpose through effort alone. It's about surrendering, being still, and allowing His love to shape you from the inside out.

THE HEART OF GOD

When we are immersed in Him, what do we feel? Protected? Accepted? All is right with the world. Nothing can phase us in that place. We know He loves us. We are forgiven. Our hearts are full, but what's next?

We are generally aware of our own hearts. What we feel, what we think. We know that out of our hearts flow the issues of life (Prov 4:23). Out of the abundance of the heart the mouth speaks (Luke 6:45).

We believe that our hearts must be right before the Lord first before we can enter into His Presence. What if we are wrong?

Isaiah 40:11 says, "He is like a shepherd feeding his flock, gathering his lambs with his arm, carrying them against his chest, gently leading the mother sheep." (CJB)

Matt 18:12-14: "What's your opinion? What will somebody do who has a hundred sheep, and one of them wanders away? Won't he leave the ninety-nine on the hillsides and go off to find the stray? And if he happens to find it? Yes! I tell you he is happier over it than over the ninety-nine that never strayed! (CJB)

The Hebrew word for lamb used in Isaiah 40:11 is tela טְלָא. It is only used once in scripture (BenTorah, 2016, pg 276). There are several other words for lamb, indicating a young lamb, a perfect lamb (w/o spot or blemish), a sacrificial lamb, etc. But this particular word actually means a wounded lamb that cannot walk or feed on its own. This lamb must be carried and hand-fed by the Shepherd. It is carried close to His heart! The 99 are left in good shape to feed from the green pastures. They don't require carrying. The wounded lamb does.

Let's look further at the heart of God.

The Hebrew word used for heart is lev or levav. These are spelled with lamed-bet (lev) or lamed-bet-bet (levav) (לֵב or לֵבָב). Levav almost always has to do with the mind, will, or emotions. The double bet is a joining together of two hearts. When you see the double bet, it can mean that your heart is joined to the heart of God (BenTorah, 2016, p. 28). Why is this important?

Song of Solomon 4:9 says "you have ravished my heart" (levav). The Heb word for ravished is לִבַּבְתִּינִ or levabetini. Levav is the root word here.

This is a picture of 2 hearts opening up to each other and becoming EQUALLY vulnerable to each other. Extrabiblical literature defines levabetini as the pulling off the bark from a tree (BenTorah, 2016, p. 28). This leaves a tree fully exposed and unprotected. God has opened His heart to us- made his heart vulnerable to us! Many of us skip Song of Solomon as being too personal or too mushy. Why is it there?

Whose heart was ravished?

We are always trying to protect our hearts, but did you know that God Himself has made His heart open and vulnerable to you? Did you know that you are responsible for protecting God's heart?

We are created in His image. That means that just as our hearts can be broken, so can His! We can experience His joy, but also His sorrow.

What breaks His heart?

We usually think about the lost, the backslidden, etc. BUT What about when we say no to Him? "Too tired, too broke, too busy". He wants to spend some time loving on us, but instead we give Him our wants and needs list, then go about our day. He says, "Come away with Me in prayer and worship", but we reluctantly give Him a few minutes, then when His Presence or the answer to our prayer doesn't manifest in our allotted time frame, we get up and leave.

Imagine what would happen to your marriage if you treated your spouse this way—giving only a little, expecting immediate results, and walking out when things don't happen as quickly as you want.

Now, consider how God must feel. He desires our hearts—not just our requests or routines—but a genuine, ongoing relationship. When we rush through prayer or dismiss His presence because we're impatient, we risk missing the depths of His love and the transformation He wants to work within us.

Love is not just toward each other as brothers and sisters in Messiah, but it is also the language of levav- an unprotected heart willing and open to others:

> *Love is incredibly patient. Love is gentle and consistently kind to all. It refuses to be jealous. Love does not brag about one's achievements nor inflate its own importance. Love does not traffic in shame and disrespect, nor selfishly seek its own honor. Love is not easily irritated or quick to take offense. Love joyfully celebrates honesty and finds no delight in what is wrong. Love is a safe place of shelter, for it never stops believ-*

ing the best for others. Love never takes failure as defeat, for it never gives up. Love never stops loving. It extends beyond the gift of prophecy, which eventually fades away. It is more enduring than tongues, which will one day fall silent. Love remains long after words of knowledge are forgotten. 1 Cor 13:4-8 (TPT)

If we truly want to see our lives transformed and our identity blossom, we must FIRST join our hearts to His, determine to never say no to Him, protect His heart at all costs, and be obedient to everything He tells us to do. Does this apply to everyone? Don't forget the tela (wounded lambs). They are accepted right where they are!

Psalm 39:1-7

I said to myself, "I will watch what I do and not sin in what I say. I will hold my tongue when the ungodly are around me." But as I stood there in silence— not even speaking of good things— the turmoil within me grew worse. The more I thought about it, the hotter I got, igniting a fire of words:

"Lord, remind me how brief my time on earth will be. Remind me that my days are numbered— how fleeting my life is. You have made my life no longer than the width of my hand. My entire lifetime is just a moment to you; at best, each of us is but a breath."

We are merely moving shadows, and all our busy rushing ends in nothing. We heap up wealth, not knowing who will spend it. And so, Lord, where do I put my hope (ka-vah')? My only hope is in you. (NLT)

TRUE LOVE KNOWS HOW TO WAIT, HOW TO HOPE.

Gen 49:18 "For Your salvation I wait, O LORD. (NASB)

Since when do we have to "wait" for salvation? Isn't it just for the asking? The Hebrew word here for "wait" is *kav-vah'*. According to Strong's Concordance (H6960), it is a primitive root meaning "to *bind* together (by *twisting*)". It is a rope or cord (a nautical term).

Other Kav-vah' scriptures:

> **Psa 27:14** *Wait for (be woven together into) the LORD; Be strong and let your heart take courage; Yes, wait for the LORD (NASB).*

> **Isa 40:31** *Yet those who wait (be woven together into) for the LORD Will gain new strength; They will mount up with wings like eagles, They will run and not get tired, They will walk and not become weary (NASB).*

Rewording Gen 49:18 from Hebrew- Yehovah, I am woven together into your Yeshua. That's a LOT different than sitting and waiting! Strength and courage come from being woven together with Yeshua!

Psa 62:5 My soul, wait in silence for God only, For my hope is from Him. (NASB)

The word for silence here is Da-mam' דָּמַם (Strong, H1826)

It means to be quiet or silent. Looking at the Hebrew letters, the Dalet (on the right) pictures a door to the letters that follow. Mem symbolizes an immersion into water (the washing of the water of the Word) and speaks of the revealed knowledge of God. Notice it is open on the bottom, allowing for a flow of revelation. The final mem (closed all the way around) speaks of the hidden knowledge of God- a place only accessible in the secret place. (BenTorah, 2018, p. 156). Yeshua is the door to this level of revelation!

Psalm 62:5 does not contain the word "wait", only silence. Hope comes from the root word kav-vah'. Restating Ps 62:5- Surely does my soul attach itself to God in a silent expectation of deep revelation from Him alone.

We can no more know who He created us to be, what we carry on our lives, and what we are to do with our lives than a new employee thrown into a job without any training or experience and without instructions from the boss. We must kav-vah' with Him.

Ancient ships used a rock with a rope attached to it as an anchor. One strand is easily broken, but many strands woven together provide tremendous strength. When all the strands are woven together with Yeshua in the mix, maximum strength is achieved when the rope is stretched in the storm! (BenTorah, 2018, p. 158). The more you are stretched in the storm, the stronger your faith becomes!

OTHER WAIT WORDS

Khool or kheel is a primitive root meaning properly to *twist* or *whirl* (in a circular or spiral manner), that is, (specifically) to *dance, to birth or bring forth (Strong, H2342).*

> **Psa 37:7-8** *Rest (Da-mam') (to hold your peace, be silent) in the LORD and wait patiently (dance to bring forth) for Him; Do not fret because of him who prospers in his way, Because of the man who carries out wicked schemes. Cease from anger and forsake wrath; Do not fret; it leads only to evildoing (NASB).*

Resting and waiting in the Lord according to Ps 37:7-8 is literally immersing oneself into the deeper things and causing oneself to dance! There is no sitting around here "waiting" for something to happen. Wait is a type of worship, and worship is a weapon of our warfare. This is actively waiting on God while stomping the devil under your feet!

Khaw-kah is a primitive root (apparently akin to H2707 (to carve) through the idea of *piercing*); properly to *adhere* to (Strong, H2442).

> *Isa 30:18* *Yet Adonai is just waiting (carved, adhered to you) to show you favor, he will have pity on you from on high; for Adonai is a God of justice; happy are all who wait for (carved into) Him! (CJB)*

He in us and us in Him! THAT'S what it means to wait.

> *Isa 49:16* *I have engraved (khaw-kak'- to engrave) you on the palms of my hands, your walls are always before me." (CJB)*

HE has carved by piercing us on HIS palms. Our walls (of protection) are always before Him. In ancient Assyria, when young men went off to war, their mothers would engrave (tattoo) their names on the palms of their hands (usually the right hand) as that symbolized being closest to the heart.

WHAT DOES ALL THIS MEAN?

Waiting is NOT waiting as we mean in English! It is NOT a passive sitting around!

We become bound together by twisting with Him, tightly woven, engraved into Him, holding our peace and keeping silent (immersed in deep revelation) in the midst of the storm and DANCE before Him to bring to birth that which He has placed on our hearts! Identity flows FROM Him and through Him!

WHAT DOES IT MEAN TO BE BOUND TOGETHER IN HIM?

Jer 13:1-7 Adonai said to me, "Go, buy yourself a linen loincloth, and wrap it around your body; but don›t soften it in water." So I bought a loincloth, as Adonai had said, and put it on. Then the word of Adonai came to me a second time: "Take the loincloth you bought and are wearing, get up, go to Parah, and hide it there in a hole in the rock." So I went and hid it in Parah, as Adonai had ordered me. A long time afterwards, Adonai said to me, "Get up, go to Parah, and recover the loincloth I ordered you to hide there." So I went to Parah and dug up the loincloth; but when I took it from the place where I had hidden it, I saw that it was ruined and useless for anything.

Jer 13:11 For just as a loincloth clings to a man's body, I made the whole house of Isra'el and the whole house of Y'hudah cling to me,' says Adonai, 'so that they could be my people, building me a name and becoming for me a source of praise and honor. But they would not listen. (CJB)

The linen loincloth is often translated as a belt, but it is actually an undergarment designed to be worn next to the body. That is how close we are to be to the Lord!

Linen was used for priestly garments, among other things. Fine linen, white and pure, is the raiment assigned to the armies in heaven following Him who is called Faithful and True (Revelation 19:14). It is a symbol of the righteousness and purity of the saints (Revelation 19:8).

Linen was cheaper and less durable when it was mixed with other yarn, such as wool and cotton. The Hebrew word *shaatnez* signified garments or cloth made of two types of thread. God forbade the Israelites to wear garments made of such materials (Lev 19:19; Deut 22:11). The linen garments of the priests not only signified purity, but also modesty:

> **Exo 28:42** *Also make for them linen shorts reaching from waist to thigh, to cover their bare flesh. (CJB)*

In Jeremiah 13, we are called to be pure and soft, living right next to God Himself. Without this level of closeness, we can't dance to birth (wait). We won't be bound together by twisting, woven together with Him (wait).

What is our part? Do we passively "wait" and "hope" as defined in English?

Wait, according to Webster's 1828 dictionary, means "to stay or rest in expectation; to stop or **remain stationary**, till the arrival of some person or event".

Hope in Webster's 1828 dictionary is "a desire of some good, accompanied with at least **a slight expectation** of obtaining it, or a belief that it is obtainable".

If we are to find our identity, are we to simply sit passively by "waiting" for some unknown event or impartation to overtake us? That's what SO many believers in Messiah do! Then those who hold onto a slight expectation of something good happening in their lives gradually lose what little hope they have, fading into the obscurity of history. The daily routine of work, bills, family, and relational stressors eat away at many of us until we grow old, lose all hope of ever accomplishing anything for the Kingdom of God, and die unfulfilled. This is NOT what Yeshua has for us! There is SO MUCH MORE!

The Biblical definition of waiting or hoping in the silent place is: Being bound together with Yeshua, tightly woven, stretched in the storm, gaining strength, immersed in deeper revelation, then dancing to bring forth to birth.

What do we get if we properly wait? Strength, endurance, vision as the eagle, deeper revelation, freedom from fear, mercy, and shalom- the peace that passes ALL understanding. We get to protect His heart and find our identity!

MEN VERSUS WOMEN- PULLING TOGETHER OR PULLING APART

CREATED IN THE VERY IMAGE OF GOD!

> *"God created man in His own image, in the image of God He created him; male and female He created them"* (Gen 1:27, NASB)

Humans were created in the very image and likeness of God. What does this mean? The Hebrew word for image or likeness is "tselem" (Strong, H6754). It is used in the context of representing something. In other words, we are called to carry the attributes of the living God on this planet- to represent HIM to the world!

Furthermore, the word *tselem* is composed of three Hebrew letters:

- **Tsade** (צ), which symbolizes righteousness,

- **Lamed** (ל), representing learning, wisdom, and understanding,
- **Mem** (מ), signifying hidden secrets and deep divine truths.

Together, these elements reveal God's original design for us: to walk in His righteousness, immersed in His wisdom and knowledge, and to reflect all this to the world around us. We are His ambassadors—bearing His character, truth, and love, shining His light into a dark world.

The Hebrew words for *male* and *female* are equally intriguing. The word for *male* derives from "zakar" (Strong, H2142), which means to remember—specifically, to remember covenant faithfulness. This points to a divine calling to remember God's promises and walk in faithfulness.

The word for *female* comes from "naqab" (Strong, H5344), which means to pierce, bore through, or designate. It speaks of purpose, intention, and divine appointment, highlighting the unique role and significance of women in God's divine plan.

GENDER IDENTITY

One of the biggest demonic attacks in our time is gender identity. Society is increasingly telling young people that they can choose their gender—if they don't like the one they were born with, they can simply change it. According to the Williams Institute (2023), approximately 0.6% of the population aged 13 and over identify as transgender. Alarmingly, the percentage of youth aged 13 to 17 identifying as transgender is three times higher than that of adults. Data from AI-generated sources reveal that, in 2011, this percentage was only 0.3%; in just over a decade, it has essentially doubled.

The consequences are devastating. Suicide ideation and actual attempts are astronomical among the LGBTQ populations. "Transgender adults have a prevalence of past-year suicide ideation that is nearly twelve times higher, and a prevalence of past-year suicide attempts that is about eighteen times higher, than the U.S. general population" (Williams Institute, 2023). The Williams Institute is a pro-LGBTQ organization and attributes these statistics to discrimination and violent treatment of these individuals.

In my view, Satan has been quietly, yet intentionally, planting lies, twisting God's truth, and sowing confusion. It began with men and women being lied to by society and parroted in pulpits across America concerning appropriate gender roles. Then the enemy successfully, like the proverbial frog in the boiling pot of water, planted thoughts in the minds of unsuspecting people, suggesting that maybe they were born the wrong gender. Notice how Satan's lies twist reality—gender assignment, which is rooted in divine design, was painted as the culprit, NOT assigned societal roles.

BEING MALE

What, then, is a man's true identity? What is embedded in his very DNA that defines him as a man?

Returning to the Hebrew root for *male*, we gain a window into God's original design. According to Bible-Hub (Strong, H2142), "The act of remembering was not merely cognitive but involved a commitment to act in accordance with what was remembered."

In other words, a man is called to remember covenantal faithfulness—and, crucially, to act on it. This isn't just about mental recall; it's about embodying and living out truth and loyalty.

What does that mean practically? Contracts are legal agreements—binding, but often breakable by either side. Covenants, however, are different. They are sealed in blood, made "until death do us part"—a sacred, unbreakable promise.

WHAT ABOUT MARRIAGE?

When a man marries a woman, he is creating a blood covenant—an eternal promise to love, cherish, and remain faithful. This covenant is rooted in God's own covenant with His people, sealed by the shed blood of Yeshua Messiah on the cross, so that we might become His bride. It's a divine, everlasting bond—*until death do us part.*

So, what is the man's initial role? It's not only to remember covenantal faithfulness but to act on it—faithfully embodying loyalty, integrity, and love in every aspect of life.

What has society sown into the hearts of men for decades, if not centuries? Marriage is often called "tying the knot," and society has long portrayed men as being "tied down." The phrase "love 'em and leave 'em" gained popularity, reflecting a view that marriage is a trap—a restriction that hinders a man's freedom. For many, a "real man" is someone who can do whatever he wants, unburdened by the responsibilities of family and commitment.

This mindset has had devastating consequences. As a result, countless children are raised in fatherless homes, lacking a male role model to teach what it means to be a man, what integrity, responsibility, and love truly look like. The absence of biblical masculinity leaves a void that the enemy seeks to fill with confusion and lies.

WHAT ELSE IS A MAN?

What is woven into the DNA of a man? Men are called to protect. For the most part, men are physically stronger than women, designed that way by God. Despite attempts by society to blur these lines, the truth remains. No matter how hard the gender confusion tries to place women in roles that demand extraordinary strength, they have not succeeded in changing the fundamental biological reality.

For example, in sports, many incidents have been reported where men "transitioning" to compete against women have used their physical advantage to dominate. The result is that the men always win where strength is required, and sometimes the women get hurt. Many places have responded by banning men from competing against women in certain sports, acknowledging the undeniable truth: those born as men generally possess greater physical strength.

Why is this the case? Because God designed men and women with unique strengths and roles, each reflecting His divine intent. Men are called to protect, to stand firm, and to lead with strength and integrity. Recognizing these truths isn't about diminishing anyone but about honoring God's creation and His divine order.

MEN AND THE KANAPH

> Num 15:38-39 (BSB). *"Speak to the Israelites and tell them that throughout the generations to come, they are to make for themselves tassels for the corners of their garments, with a blue cord on each tassel. These will serve as tassels for you to look at, so that you may remember all the commandments of the LORD, that you may*

*obey them and not prostitute yourselves by fol-
lowing your own heart and your own eyes."*

Why are the tassels or the tzitzit, as they are commonly
known, so important? Are they simply reminders to
keep God's Word- That we are Holy to the Lord, or is
there more significance to this garment with its var-
ied parts and pieces? The tzitzit is attached to the four
corners of the tallit or prayer shawl. The four corners
are the "kanaph". By now, you are thinking "so much
Hebrew". Where are we going with this?

We are stepping into the protected place. The definition of "kanaph" is "wing, edge, extremity, corner". More
importantly, it comes from an unused root meaning to
cover or hide (Strong, H3671).

This imagery is powerful. The kanaph represents more
than just a physical corner; it symbolizes divine protection, covering, and the place of refuge. When we
wear the tzitzit, we are reminded of our calling to dwell
under God's protection—the wing of His covering—and
to walk in obedience, shielded by His divine presence.

"In ancient Hebrew culture, the concept of "kanaph"
was rich with symbolism. Wings were often associated with protection and refuge, as birds shelter their
young under their wings. The corners of garments, or
"kanaph," held significance in Jewish tradition, particu-
larly in the wearing of the "tallit," a prayer shawl with
fringes (tzitzit) on its corners" (Bible Hub, H3671). These
fringes were attached to the kanaph.

Psalm 91:4 (CJB) states, *"he will cover you with His pinions, and under His wings you will find refuge; His truth is a shield and protection"*. The word for wings is kanaph. Note that His truth is what places us there.

BenTorah (2018) states, "kanaph comes from an old Persian word which has the idea of guards thrusting the people or objects they are protecting into a corner and then spreading their arms around the individuals or objects, placing themselves as a human shield for their protection". God is our kanaph. He created men to be like Him.

"Let me dwell in Your tent forever; Let me take refuge in the shelter of Your wings." (Ps 61:4, NASB). Again, wings is Kanaph. To dwell in His tent means to live as a stranger, an alien in a land that is not our own (Strong, H1481). As followers of Yeshua, we are indeed strangers and sojourners in this world. Our true home is with Him. Here on Earth, we serve as kingdom ambassadors, called to advance His righteousness and bring His kingdom culture to every corner of the planet. All of this—the protection, the refuge, the divine covering—is woven into the DNA of a man. It's part of our divine design. We are created to reflect God's protective nature, to stand as guardians and providers, carrying His wings of healing and safety.

In fact, we're laying hold of healing through this divine attribute. Malachi 4:2 reminds us that Messiah comes with "healing in His wings". The Hebrew word for wings here again is kanaph. In first-century tradition, the fringes of the tzitzit were believed to possess healing power—an ancient reminder that divine protection and healing are intertwined with our identity and purpose in Messiah (Stern, 2021, p. 1400).

In Luke 8:43-48, we read about a woman who had suffered from a hemorrhage for twelve years—an affliction that no one could heal. She came up behind Yeshua and touched the tzitzit on His robe. Instantly, her hemorrhaging stopped. When Yeshua asked, "Who touched me?" the disciples, bewildered by the crowd's jostling, responded, "Rabbi! The crowds are pressuring you from all sides!" But Yeshua knew someone had touched Him with faith.

The woman, trembling with fear, stepped forward and confessed her act, explaining her long ordeal and how she was instantly healed. Yeshua looked at her with compassion and said, "My daughter, your trust has saved you; go in peace."

This woman's story reveals profound truths. She was not simply seeking physical healing; she was branded **unclean**—an outcast, isolated by law and society. She couldn't be with others at the well or in the synagogue, because even the accidental touch of her unclean body could contaminate others. For twelve long years, she sought every remedy, but nothing worked. She was drowning in hopelessness, feeling forsaken.

Then, Yeshua entered her world. Everywhere He went, He brought healing—lepers were cleansed, the blind received sight. And now, her moment had come. She believed that if she could only touch His tzitzit, she would be healed. Driven by desperation and faith, she pressed through the crowd, risking everything. If only she could touch His garment, she thought, she would be protected by His divine kanaph and made whole.

But her act exposed her. She was vulnerable. Yet instead of rebuke, Yeshua called her out, not to shame her but to affirm her faith. He covered her with His love, called her **His daughter**, and released her into peace.

Protection. Covering. Healing. These aren't just physical gifts; they are divine promises woven into the very fabric of our faith. We, as strangers in a foreign land, are waiting for our wedding with the Messiah—the Bridegroom of the universe. We are sowing seeds, investing talents, and trusting in His protection until He returns.

Ruth 3:9 (BSB) says, *"Who are you?" he asked. "I am your servant Ruth," she replied. "Spread the corner (Kanaph) of your garment over me, for you are a kinsman-redeemer."*

Ruth was most certainly a foreigner in a foreign land. She didn't know the customs or the culture, but she trusted Naomi. Naomi, understanding both the Word of the Lord as well as her culture, instructed Ruth as follows:

"Wash yourself, put on perfume, and wear your best clothes. Go down to the threshing floor, but

do not let the man know you are there until he has finished eating and drinking. When he lies down, note the place where he lies. Then go in and uncover his feet, and lie down, and he will explain to you what you should do" (Ruth 3:3-4, BSB).

Ruth was obedient to Naomi's instructions. Boaz followed suit, covered, protected, and provided for Ruth, who went on to become the great-grandmother of King David!

Men, you are designed to protect. You are designed to cover. You are designed to walk holy to the Lord and remember the covenants you cut with both the Lord and your wife.

The Kanaph covers the mercy seat of God! Ex 25:20. How are you treating the women God has placed in your care? Your wife? Your daughters? Your sisters in Messiah? Are you browbeating them into submission, or are you merciful to them? If we are to walk in His image, then mercy must be at the heart of our character. That divine image is love. It manifests in kindness, compassion, and gentle strength.

But where does strength and toughness fit into this divine picture? Never forget—the enemy is out there. Satan is prowling, seeking whom he may devour. As men of God, we must show strength and courage. We must stand firm in prayer, in truth, and in righteousness. And to the enemy, we are called to show no mercy. We are to be bold, fearless, and unwavering. The strength of a man rooted in God's mercy and love is a formidable force; one that resists darkness and advances the kingdom of light.

What happens when the kanaph is lost? When the divine covering—the kanaph—is lost, the consequences are severe. It's a warning that the protection, favor, and divine authority of God have been withdrawn. This is precisely what happened to King Saul.

In 1 Samuel 15, God commanded Saul to utterly destroy the Amalekites and their possessions. Instead, Saul spared King Agag and kept the best of the spoils, claiming to do so for sacrifice. When Samuel confronted Saul, he delivered a stark warning: God was rejecting him as king. Saul's response was not true repentance but fear of what the people would think.

As Samuel turned to leave, Saul seized the edge of his robe—the kanaph—and tore it. Samuel immediately understood the significance: Saul had torn the kanaph, symbolizing that God's divine covering and protection were being ripped away from him. Samuel declared, "The LORD has torn the kingdom of Israel from you today and has given it to your neighbor, who is better than you" (1 Samuel 15:28, NASB). The tearing of the robe was a prophetic sign—Saul's spiritual covering was gone.

Fast forward to 1 Sam 24:4: *"The men of David said to him, "Behold, this is the day of which the LORD said to you,*

'Behold; I am about to give your enemy into your hand, and you shall do to him as it seems good to you.'" Then David arose and cut off the edge of Saul's robe secretly" (NASB). David cut off Saul's kanaph! Not only did Saul realize that David could have taken his life at any time, but he was reminded once again that God's covering, His protection, was gone. Saul subsequently fell in battle, and the kingdom was given to David.

Men, woven into your very DNA, your identity, is a driving force to provide for and protect those God has entrusted to you. You are called to be a shield, a defender, a warrior standing firm in faith and courage.

Don't stand afar off, watching your wife face the enemy alone. Don't let her bear the burden of spiritual battles without your support. Man up! Step into your God-ordained role as the warrior of your family. Be the one who rises to slay the dragon, the serpent, or whatever form the enemy takes.

Remember, you are created in the image of the Almighty—strength, courage, and love are part of your divine design. It's time to rise up, take your rightful position, and fight for your household with boldness and faith. The enemy's schemes are no match for a man who walks in the authority of God.

BEING FEMALE

Have you ever felt confined, placed in a box that doesn't fit who you truly are? Perhaps you're serving in the nursery, caring for children, or assisting in ways that feel limiting. Maybe you've been assigned to teach women or children, yet deep inside, you sense there is more, something greater God has called you to.

Historically, society and religious traditions have placed women into specific roles—cooking, cleaning, caring for family, and others, while restricting them from leadership positions like teachers, pastors, or preachers. This restriction has often been rooted in a misinterpretation of Scripture, creating a legalistic box that limits women's divine calling.

The few women who dared to step outside those boundaries and answer God's true purpose faced opposition and sacrifice. Yet, history shows that God's plan for women is not confined to traditional roles. Instead, He designed women with strength, wisdom, influence, and a prophetic voice that can shape nations and impact eternity.

God's purpose for women is not meant to be boxed in by human tradition or misunderstanding. You are fearfully and wonderfully made, created in the image of God to reflect His strength, grace, and authority. When you embrace your divine purpose, you walk in the fullness of His calling, whether in leadership, teaching, prophecy, or service.

WHAT'S OUR TRUE IDENTITY AS WOMEN OF GOD?

In today's America, identity has become a major battleground. Yet, in many third-world nations, people face struggles like hunger, war, and lack of freedom. Interestingly, the real war here isn't over resources or politics; it's over identity. Who are we really? Who does God say we are? Yeshua addressed this question directly.

> *When Jesus came to the region of Caesarea Philippi, He questioned His disciples: "Who do people say the Son of Man is?"*
>
> *They replied, "Some say John the Baptist; others say Elijah; and still others, Jeremiah or one of the prophets."*
>
> *"But what about you?" Jesus asked. "Who do you say I am?"*
>
> *Simon Peter answered, "You are the Christ, the Son of the living God."*
>
> *Jesus replied, "Blessed are you, Simon son of Jonah! For this was not revealed to you by flesh and blood, but by My Father in heaven. And I tell you that you are Peter, and on this rock I will build My church, and the gates of Hades will not prevail against it. I will give you the keys of the kingdom of heaven. Whatever you bind on earth will*

be bound in heaven, and whatever you loose on earth will be loosed in heaven." (Matt 16:13-19, BSB).

What is "the rock" that Jesus speaks of? When He asks, "Who do YOU say that I am?", He's not merely seeking a confession of faith—He's confronting us with a question about HIS identity and the subsequent foundation of our lives.

The rock isn't just a symbol; it's the firm, unshakable foundation, Yeshua Himself. He is the cornerstone upon which everything must be built. A house constructed on this solid rock can withstand the fiercest storms. Conversely, a house built on shifting sand—on societal opinions, fleeting trends, or personal feelings - will inevitably crumble when life's storms hit (Luke 6:48-49).

Today, the shifting sands are more unstable than ever. Public opinion is constantly changing, questioning gender, identity, morality, and even reality itself. What was once considered mental illness is now normalized in some circles. And tomorrow? Who knows what new "truths" the world will promote?

But as women and men of God, our identity must be anchored in Yeshua, our Lord and Messiah. Anything else, any fleeting trend, societal label, or cultural opinion, will crumble under pressure. We cannot carry the keys of authority, purchased for us through the cross, and storm the gates of hell unless our identity is rooted in Him, not in who the world says we are.

EZER KENEGDO

Gen 2:18 (BSB) *"The LORD God also said, "It is not good for the man to be alone. I will make for him a suitable helper."* An Ezer Kenegdo.

What exactly is a helper, an ezer (Strong, H5828)? In ancient times, Most activities, eating, fellowship, etc., were done in the courtyard of the house, under the stars, where nothing obstructed our view of or access to God. The word Ezer is usually translated as a help or helper. This Hebrew word is also used to describe a courtyard, but not ANY courtyard! It's used to describe the courtyard of the Tabernacle! This is the place where the atmosphere is shifted and the man is prepared to meet with God.

Therefore, the woman was created to be more than just a helper; she's designed to assist the man in drawing closer to God. A better translation might be "help to meet" - someone who helps facilitate divine encounter and spiritual intimacy.

The word Kenegdo (Strong, H5048) means "in front of," "opposite," or "in sight of." Often, it describes someone who goes before you, yet remains in your presence—a protector, a battle-partner, an armor-bearer. It comes from a root word meaning "to stand boldly to expose," often used in military contexts for aid in battle.

In essence, Kenegdo signifies someone who stands with you—boldly, in front of you, and in your sight—serving as both a shield and a guide, helping you meet with God and fight the battles of life.

In Gen 2:18, the word "alone" is separated from someone or something. The prefix for "a" is not in the text.

This scripture could read: *It is not good for man to be separated. I will make out of him someone to stand before him as an armor bearer, an atmosphere shifter, to help him meet with God and fight the battle before him!* (Gen 2:18, Sho version 😄)

In Gen 2:21-22, God takes a "rib" from Adam to make Eve. This is the Hebrew word "tsela" meaning "side". *Tsela* (Strong, H6763) is used 41 times in the Old Testament, and only two times is it rendered as a rib (BenTorah, 2024).

It comes from the Hebrew root word "tsala" meaning to limp. Literally "to limp (as if one-sided)." According to rabbinical commentary, they believe that Adam was actually cut in half and 2 people were created out of the one.

We women are unique in that ALL other animals were created separately from their male counterparts (Gen 1:24-25). Adam was created as a one-sided being, a complete, whole man. From that wholeness, God formed woman, not as a lesser creature but as the other half of divine wholeness.

Who else ended up with a limp? Jacob.

In Genesis 32:24 (BSB), we read, "Jacob was left all alone, and there a man wrestled with him until daybreak." The word *"alone"* here signifies being separate, isolated. During this intense encounter, Jacob's hip is dislocated—he walks away forever marked with a limp, a *tsala*.

Would God do this? Yes. Sometimes, in our most distressing moments, God allows us to experience a limp—an injury or weakness—that becomes a reminder of a divine encounter. Jacob's limp was not a sign of defeat but a symbol of divine sovereignty. It was a tangible object lesson—an object lesson in God's design and authority.

Who was Jacob afraid of? He was afraid of man—his brother Esau, enemies, or circumstances. Yet, in his greatest distress, Jacob separated himself from his family, sending his wives and children ahead, while he isolated himself. He chose to wrestle alone, away from the safety of others, away from his armor bearer.

But in that wrestling, Jacob learned an essential truth: to fear God, not man. When he named the place Peniel, saying, *"I have seen God face to face, and my life has been preserved"* (Gen 32:30), it marked a turning point. His encounter with God changed him—he left with a new identity, a new fear, and a new purpose.

Ladies, here's the divine insight: Without women, men often walk with a limp—weak, incomplete, or vulnerable. Women are the divine counterparts who help men walk in wholeness, strength, and a divine fear of the Lord.

Where else is Ezer used?

In Deuteronomy 33:29, the Lord Himself is described as *"magen ezer,"* often translated as "shield and helper." But interestingly, the Hebrew text contains no conjunction—no "and." It simply states that God is our shield who stands before us.

If the Creator of the universe describes Himself as an Ezer, ladies, that elevates your divine calling to a high and sacred level. You are not merely helpers in the human sense; you are designed to reflect God's own protective, guiding, and empowering nature.

In John 14:26, Yeshua speaks of the Helper (Greek: Paraclete), saying:

> *"But the Helper, the Holy Spirit, whom the Father will send in My name, He will teach you all things and bring to your remembrance all that I said to you" (NASB).*

The Greek Paraclete is more than just a helper; it's a warrior companion, originally used in ancient Greece to describe a fellow warrior assigned to fight back-to-back with you. Your Paraclete stands with you, protecting you from unseen enemies, fighting alongside you so that the enemy cannot sneak up from behind.

WHAT ELSE DOES THE WORD SAY ABOUT WOMEN?

1 Peter 3:7 (NASB 1977) says: *"You husbands likewise, live with your wives in an understanding way, as with a weaker vessel, since she is a woman; and grant her honor as a fellow heir of the grace of life, so that your prayers may not be hindered"*.

Context is key:

> *1 Peter 3:1-6 (NASB): Likewise, wives, be subject to your own husbands, so that even if some do not obey the word, they may be won without a word by the conduct of their wives, when they see your respectful and pure conduct. Do not let your adorning be external—the braiding of hair and the putting on of gold jewelry, or the clothing you wear— but let your adorning be the hidden person of the heart with the imperishable beauty of a gentle and quiet spirit, which in God's sight is very precious. For this is how the holy women who hoped in God used to adorn themselves, by submitting to their own husbands, as Sarah obeyed Abraham, calling him*

lord. And you are her children, if you do good and do not fear anything that is frightening.

What does it mean to be "subject"? It is usually translated as "submit or be subject". It is the Greek word (Strong, G52930) hoopo-tas'-so, meaning to rank under, to obey, submit, put myself into subjection. From hupo meaning "by or under" and tasso meaning "to put in order or arrange.

Eph 5:21 (BSB): Submit to one another out of reverence (reverential respect & awe) for Christ. The word submit is hoopo-tas'-so.

Let's look at another passage of scripture concerning the word submit:

> *Eph 5:22-24 (BSB) Wives, submit to your husbands as to the Lord. For the husband is the head of the wife as Christ is the head of the church, His body, of which He is the Savior. Now, as the church submits to Christ, so also wives should submit to their husbands in everything.*

The word submit isn't even in the original language! It was added by the English translators. It should read "Wives, be to your husbands as to the Lord".

A related word is hoop-ak-oo'-o (Strong, G5219), meaning to listen to attentively to obey. It is the word used for obedience to the gospel, slaves to their masters, or in a negative connotation, your flesh obeying the call of sin. The wind and seas obeyed Yeshua (Matt 8:27). The spirits obeyed Him (Mark 1:27). Hoopakoo'o.

So what's the difference? Huppotasso is a choice made to arrange oneself in order with another for the purpose of protection! Hoopakoo'o is more of a commanded obedience. I choose to be arranged (Huppotasso) with my husband for protection and to do life with. I am not his slave (Hoopakoo'o) to be bossed around, beaten, or abused.

In the Jewish wedding, the bride & groom are married under a huppa, a covering. As they are united together under the covering protection of God, the husband provides a covering protection for his wife. He provides a kanaph.

> Ruth 3:7-9 (BSB): *After Boaz had finished eating and drinking and was in good spirits, he went to lie down at the end of the heap of grain. Then Ruth went in secretly, uncovered his feet, and lay down. At midnight, Boaz was startled, turned over, and there lying at his feet was a woman! "Who are you?" he asked. "I am your servant Ruth," she replied. "Spread the corner of your garment over me, for you are a kinsman-redeemer."*

Why would Ruth uncover his feet, then ask him to cover her? Ruth originally introduces herself as a maidservant (*shiphachah*) in Ruth 2:13, but then as a maidservant (*amah*) in Ruth 3:9. What's the difference?

A *shipachah* is a housemaid who has served her master so well that she feels a part of the family or is an actual family member who serves as a maid or servant (BenTorah, 2019). This is NOT someone eligible to marry the master. Ruth, as a foreigner, felt she was not eligible to marry an Israelite. Naomi instructed her in the ways of Torah. She now saw herself as an amah-someone who is eligible for marriage with the master. She uncovers his feet (something a prostitute might do), but instead of asking a price, she requests his covering! His protection! His Kanaph!

We were ALL prostitutes! Not eligible to be the bride of Messiah, but Yeshua changed all that! He covered us as our kinsman redeemer! Two different women uncovered and anointed Yeshua's feet. He covered them both! What is a kinsman-redeemer? A perfect picture of Messiah!

When you intentionally and respectfully place yourself under your husband's leadership, you are stepping into a divine calling. God has given him a command—to protect, lead, and cherish you. At the same time, you have a divine mandate to honor and respect him.

This isn't about blind obedience or submission to every whim. Instead, it's about honoring his role as the head, as unto the Lord. You show respect not because he is perfect, but because God has established divine order in marriage.

Respect and honor mean talking with him, spending quality time, listening, and supporting him as a partner. It's about allowing him to be the man God designed him to be—protector, provider, spiritual leader—without trying to control or fix every situation in your own strength. When disagreements arise over decisions, the key is to bring those concerns before the Lord, trusting His wisdom and timing. You are called to be a helper, not a fixer, trusting God to guide your husband and your marriage.

1 Peter 3:7 says:

> *"You husbands likewise, live with your wives in an understanding way, as with a weaker vessel, since she is a woman; and grant her honor as a fellow heir of the grace of life, so that your prayers may not be hindered"* (NASB 1977).

Understanding or knowledge is the Greek word (Strong, G1097) "ginóskó" which means an intimate, deep knowing. This is a personal experiential knowing, NOT just knowing something about someone.

WHAT ABOUT "WEAKER VESSEL"?

Greek translates weaker vessel as... weaker vessel. So... what's up with that?

In Greek, the words weaker vessel are asthenestero skevel. Asthenestero comes from the root word asthenes, which means to be delicate, weak, sickly, infirmed, without strength, and/or unimpressive. Skevel is the word for a vessel which doesn't help this politically incorrect situation at all because it means property, merchandise, or goods that are carried in a vessel. In other words, Greek says that ladies are a delicate piece of merchandise!

Another problem is that the rhetoric and philosophy expressed in this letter suggest someone with a formal education, which Peter did not have. Peter spoke an Old Galilean form of Aramaic, which was a colloquial and backwater-type language (BenTorah, 2022).

Peter had his personal scribe, Silvanus, not only write the letter but also translate it for Peter into Greek to be sent to the Greek churches of Asia Minor. This creates the problem of whether Silvanus's translation of Peter's letter from the Aramaic is the inspired Word of God or was Peter's Aramaic version the inspired Word of God (BenTorah, 2022).

The word for vessel in Aramaic is mana, which is a word for garments or clothes. Its root comes from a Phoenician origin for the outriggers of a ship. The outriggers of a ship are what keep the ship on course and moving. Without it, the ship is dead in the water. So this vessel idea is really speaking of a ship and the outrigging of a ship. The outrigging includes the sails, which power the ship, and the rudders that guide and navigate the ship. It would be fitting for a former fisherman to use a seafaring illustration. Thus, the word for weak in Aramaic is the word machal, which means weak, but weak only in the sense of paying off a debt to a debtor so he has no power over you and is weakened. Machal is more of the idea of neutralizing a threat (BenTorah, 2022).

Following a nautical motif, when the word machal to neutralize a threat is used as an adjective for the word mana, the outrigging of a ship, it would express the idea of a wife who is the outrigging of the vessel her husband. When the storms of life come, the sailor uses the outrigging, the anchor, the rudder, and the sails to steer the ship in such a way as to weather out the storm. Without the outrigging, the vessel is dead in the water and subject to whatever currents come its way. It has no direction. With the mana, the outrigging or a man's wife, the man has direction and the power to follow that direction. When the storms of life come, the wife and husband work together to navigate and ride out the storm (BenTorah, 2022).

PUTTING IT ALL TOGETHER

When women's identity is rooted firmly in Messiah, they fully understand what it means to be covered by Him and the men God has placed in their lives. This divine foundation sets women free to be the help-meets, atmosphere shifters, armor bearers, and vital components of an unstoppable team. Women are called to create an environment where God's presence reigns—a sacred atmosphere where divine encounters happen, and spiritual battles are won.

Men, in turn, understand their divine calling to provide, protect, and wage spiritual warfare. They are equipped to carry heavy loads, to fight on behalf of their families, and to expect their wives to hand off the right weapon at precisely the right moment. Together, they ascend into the throne room of God through worship—creating an atmosphere of divine authority—and descend into the battlefield, fully equipped and ready for war.

Women trust their husbands to lead and protect, while men trust their wives to navigate the storm. Together, they form an unbreakable, divinely anointed team. This divine order, this unity, is exactly what the enemy fights tooth and toenail. Because he knows that when God's design is fully embraced—when men and women walk in their divine roles—nothing can stand against God's purpose.

THE RELAY RACE

Have you ever participated in a relay race? There's a baton that each team member carries through their portion of the race. The first runner starts strong, runs their segment, and then must hand off the baton smoothly to the next teammate. This hand-off is crucial; it can make or break the race. The success depends on flawless practice until the transfer becomes second nature. If the baton is dropped, the race is almost certainly lost.

Every team member must train diligently, perfecting their part. Otherwise, the entire team suffers. If one person is consistently late for practice or doesn't put their full effort into training, they risk being dropped from the team altogether. The race requires unity, discipline, and precision.

Sometimes, we listen to voices within that undermine our confidence. "You're not good enough." "They don't really want you; they're just being polite." "Your part isn't important." Conversely, some voices whisper,

"You're too talented for these people." "They're just keeping you in the background so they can shine."

When we bow before the "god of me," we drop the baton every time. Instead of repenting and refocusing, we blame ourselves or others. We become distant from the people God has placed in our lives to protect, guide, and support us.

The enemy eagerly seizes this separation, the rift, the division, and moves in for the kill. The enemy's goal is to disrupt the unity, to cause us to drop the baton, and to divide the body of Messiah.

REPAIRING THE BREACH

When there's a breach in the body—a cut or wound—it bleeds. If the bleeding isn't stopped, it will lead to hemorrhaging. The life is in the blood. Unchecked, the blood flows out, and the body begins to die. This truth applies both physically and spiritually.

In the physical body, specialized blood components come into action to stem the flow. When a breach occurs, platelets—tiny but vital cells—rush to the scene. Normally, they circulate smoothly, but at the site of injury, they become rough on their surfaces. This change allows them to trap clotting factors, forming a fibrin mesh that creates a clot, sealing the wound and stopping the bleed.

Platelets are produced in the bone marrow from stem cells as needed. They are one of three main types of blood cells:

- Red blood cells carry oxygen to every part of the body and remove carbon dioxide—these are the primary carriers of life.
- White blood cells are the warriors—fighting infection and defending the body from harm.
- Platelets help stop the bleeding, maintaining the integrity of the body.

"The function of the coagulation pathway is to keep hemostasis, which is the blockage of a bleeding or hemorrhage. Primary hemostasis is an aggregation of platelets forming a plug at the damaged site of exposed endothelial cells. Secondary hemostasis includes the two main coagulation pathways, intrinsic and extrinsic, that meet up at a point to form the common pathway. The common pathway ultimately activates fibrinogen into fibrin. These fibrin subunits have an affinity for each other and combine into fibrin strands that bind the platelets together, stabilizing the platelet plug" (Chaudhry, Usama, & Babiker, 2023).

I realize this is a lot, so let me explain. Platelets are the first guys at the scene of an injury. They get sticky, change shape, and clump together to plug the hole. They then activate the rest of the clotting mechanisms to come running to assist. Platelets can't stop the bleed by themselves. They MUST change their shape so they can stick together.

Two pathways combine into one common pathway. All along these pathways, different clotting factors are activated and, in turn, activate the next one, and so on. If one of these factors is missing, such as in hemophilia, the rest of the cascade is NOT activated, and the bleed continues. Think of it like a relay race: each factor activates the next, passing the baton until the process is complete.

Most of these factors are identified by Roman numerals, but two are named after the person who discovered them. One of them is called the Christmas factor! They form different subunits that love each other. These combine into strands and bind the platelets together to form a mesh. The mesh links to the sides of the breach, pulling it together, forming a clot (or a scab if you prefer), healing the wound. Other guys (factors) patrol the area, keeping the clot from getting too big, and then send signals when the wound is healed and it's time for the clot to dissolve.

HOW DOES THIS FIT SPIRITUALLY?

We are the Body of Messiah. Yeshua must be at the center—without Him, we risk bleeding out spiritually. All of us are interconnected, whether we realize it or not. We are called to support one another, to love fiercely, and to work together in unity. Just like in our physical bodies, where cuts and wounds happen unexpectedly, rifts and breaches also develop within Messiah's body.

The key members, those who recognize the tear first, must rush to plug the hole. But they can't heal the rift alone. They need to change shape—becoming sticky—so they can adhere to the site of injury. They activate others, calling them to rush to the scene, to do their part, and to help heal the wound.

The question is: How many times have believers identified a breach—a tear or rift—and instead of helping, they refuse to open themselves up, making themselves vulnerable? How often do we pull away from the bleeding person, refusing to stick to them or to offer help? Instead, we criticize or judge the one bleeding, refusing to get close enough to care and support.

Gal 5:15 says, *"But if you keep on biting and devouring one another, watch out, or you will be consumed by one another" (BSB).*

The bleeding continues... Those who are gifted to help, who are positioned to help, are never activated to help. They are not positioned. Leaders: When it doesn't make sense, ESPECIALLY when it doesn't make sense, position key people anyway. You can't do this by yourself!

OUR INITIAL POSITION DETERMINES EVERYONE ELSE'S ROLE

Just like in the physical body, our initial position when we see a breach sets the course for healing. Remember, platelets are not born from other platelets; they originate from stem cells that become platelets as the body needs them. When you recognize a rift—a wound or division—run to the person bleeding, stick close, and begin the healing process.

For true healing to occur spiritually, all the clotting factors must be activated. This isn't a solo effort. Intercessors must rush to the site of the injury, praying fervently, binding the forces of darkness—those inhibitors that try to prevent the clot from forming. Prophetic giftings are vital here, providing divine understanding of where the rift is and what caused it. They help build clarity on how to proceed.

As the word of the breach spreads, each factor, each believer, each gift, must be activated and mobilized. These factors then activate others, creating a chain reaction with ONE COMMON GOAL: to heal the rift and restore unity.

Imagine a divine network where every part plays its role—from prayer warriors to prophets, from leaders to everyday believers. When each one recognizes their position and steps into their God-ordained role, the entire body works together seamlessly. The activation of one causes others to follow, creating a powerful wave of healing that aligns with God's purpose.

Spiritually, this process mirrors how healing and restoration happen in the body of Messiah. When we see a breach, we must run to the scene, stick close, and activate others—praying, declaring, prophesying, and standing in faith. Together, we form a divine coagulation, an unbreakable bond, designed to stop the hemorrhage and bring lasting healing.

What does the word say?

> *Eph 6:12 says, "For our struggle is not against flesh and blood, but against the rulers, against the authorities, against the powers of this world's darkness, and against the spiritual forces of evil in the heavenly realms" (BSB).*

There are OUTSIDE forces at work to tear us apart! They are subtle and devious. They make us think that the problem comes from within. "It's THAT person's fault. What were they thinking? They should not have done that"!

Jesus said, *"I in them and You in Me—that they may be perfectly united, so that the world may know that You sent Me and have loved them just as You have loved Me"* (John 17:23, BSB).

What?!? Perfectly united?? The word united here means to be ONE. NO division. The same as the Hebrew "echad". The word used to describe the relationship between the Father, Son, and Spirit. Perfectly means to accomplish, to complete, to finish, to bring to the goal. This is not a mental assent, nor a verbal agreement with everything said. This is a level of love, an affinity for one another that says, "I'm going to pull alongside you so you don't bleed all over the place and the world knows we are HIS.

James 1:4 says, *"Allow perseverance to finish its work, so that you may be mature and complete, not lacking anything"* (BSB). Perseverance leads to maturity. Maturity provides a sheltered environment.

"Fibrin formation thus occurs in the sheltered environment of the platelet membrane, where it is localized to the site of injury and protected from circulating inhibitors" (Green, 2006).

Are you a restorer, a repairer of the breach? Are you called to be a platelet? When YOU detect a rift in the local body of Messiah where you are planted, what is your response? Do you rush to the site of the injury, open yourself up so you can gather the troops, protect them during the repair job, and activate others to do their part?

Do you go into self-protection mode and distance yourself from the breach, waiting to see what happens? Do you partner with the inhibitors, exposing the wound, preventing healing from taking place by spreading gossip?

Matt 7:1 says, *"Judge not, or you will be judged"* (BSB)

Gossip and slander in the church doesn't usually look like "did you hear what so and so did"? It's often based in reality rather than overt lies. It says, "This is just so you can pray about this". "We need to pray for so and so; they are under attack". Notice I said reality, not truth. These are two different things. Reality is perceptual and personal. Truth comes from and is based in Yeshua and His Word.

THE DIFFERENCE BETWEEN REALITY AND TRUTH

Many years ago, during a time of fasting and prayer, I found myself at a retreat center nestled in the mountains. As I looked out the window, my eyes caught a mountainside covered in lush evergreen trees, with a small utility building nestled among them. Suddenly, a thick fog began to roll in. It grew increasingly dense until I was completely engulfed, unable to see anything other than this impenetrable cloud of mist.

Then I heard the Lord speak softly, "What do you see?"
I responded, "I see a thick fog."
He asked again, "But what is really there?"
I responded with, "A mountainside with trees and a small building."

The Lord then said, "This is the difference between reality and truth."

"Reality is what you perceive, what your eyes see, what your feelings tell you. It's based on your external circumstances, on what appears to be true in the moment. But My truth is different. It is immovable and unshakable.

It remains constant regardless of what your senses tell you or what the fog of life tries to obscure".

"When you find yourself immersed in the fog of life—confusion, doubt, fear—do not base your decisions solely on what your eyes see or your feelings feel. Instead, anchor yourself in My truth. Trust what I say about your situation, about your life, about your future. Because, in Me, there is clarity—there is light beyond the fog".

How are you running the race that's been set before you? When a teammate stumbles and falls, do you point the finger at them, accusing them of costing you the race, or do you stop, pick them up, and help them to the finish line?

I will ask you again: Are you a restorer, a repairer of the breach, or are you increasing the bleed? God has gifted us with the tools to repair the rifts as they arise. The enemy wants us to bleed out!

THE BIG LIE

It's not my fault. It's their fault. They don't understand me. The pastor isn't who I thought he was. The leadership staff doesn't care about me. I can't trust the sheep- they bite! I've had enough. I refuse ever to trust anyone ever again. I don't need anyone else. I can do this myself!

Do any of these statements sound familiar? Have YOU said any of these things? I want you to know that NONE of these statements has any basis in scripture. They are, in fact, lies from the pit of hell to get you to separate yourself from your brothers and sisters in Christ, so it's easier for the devil to pick you off!

I recently watched a documentary about a herd of water buffalo being attacked by a couple of lionesses. Water buffalo are large, formidable animals—dangerous in their own right. Lions, knowing this, typically target the young, the weak, or the stragglers—those outside the safety of the herd's defense.

The lions don't attack those running in the middle of the pack. Why? Because the herd forms a protective circle, horns facing outward, creating a nearly impenetrable barrier. The lions cannot break through this defense without risking injury—they know their limits.

However, there was a young water buffalo that had wandered just a little bit away from the herd, far enough that it couldn't catch up once the attack began. Isolated, vulnerable, it was quickly overtaken and brought down.

This scene echoes a powerful spiritual truth found in 1 Peter 5:8:

> *"Be sober-minded and alert. Your adversary the devil prowls around like a roaring lion, seeking someone to devour."* (BSB)

What does it mean to be sober-minded? The basic definition is not to be intoxicated. Seems pretty simple, but of course, there's more! The Greek word ne'pho (G3525) is used here, and it also means to keep watch, be discreet, and be free from illusion. It's not enough to abstain from mind-altering addictions, but we must be vigilant and RUN from selfish passions, run from greed, run from everything that hurts God's heart. If we choose to dabble even a tiny amount in these things, we give the enemy legal access. God wants to protect us from these things, but the devil is a legalist and will demand judgment until we repent and apply the blood sacrifice of Jesus.

Be alert is just that. Awaken! Watch! Be vigilant! Stay alert!

> *"But be sure of this, that if the head of the house had known at what time of the night the thief was coming, he would have been on the alert and would not have allowed his house to be broken into"* (Matt 24:43, NASB). The same Greek word is used in both 1 Peter 5:8 as well as Matt 24:43.

HOW DO WE KEEP FROM BEING ATTACKED AND DEVOURED?

It begins with being sober-minded—alert and aware of the spiritual realities around us. It starts with walking close to Yeshua, staying connected to His Word and His presence. Equally important is living in community with others.

Most of us aren't taken out by the demon we see. Instead, we fall prey to the one we don't see—the subtle, hidden attack that comes when we're isolated. Just like the young buffalo that wandered away from the herd, when we stray from the safety of fellowship, prayer, and accountability—when we disconnect from the protective presence of God and His people—we become vulnerable.

When we walk close to the Lord and stay in community, angelic warriors surround us. They guard us, and others in the body of Messiah can often see the attack before we do. When in trusted relationships, others have permission to speak into our lives, warning us of approaching danger, helping us face the enemy before he overtakes us.

But what about the hurt and betrayal? Many say, "You don't understand what they did to me. How can I ever trust again?" Jesus addresses this heartache directly. He says, *"For if you forgive men their trespasses, your heavenly Father will also forgive you. But if you do not forgive men their trespasses, neither will your Father forgive your trespasses"* (Matthew 6:14-15, BSB).

And Peter, seeking clarity, asks Jesus, *"Lord, how often shall my brother sin against me, and I forgive him? Up to seven times?" Jesus responds, "I do not say to you, up to seven times, but up to seventy times seven"* (Matthew 18:21-22, NASB).

Are you perfect? Do you ever make mistakes? Do you know anyone on this planet (besides Holy Spirit) who is perfect? I didn't think so. Quit worshipping the "god of me" and instead worship the God who loves you and knows you better than you know yourself. Worship the One who said, "Father, forgive them. They know not what they do" (Luke 23:34).

We should know this, yet we get butt-hurt about something and allow the enemy to get in our heads. We rehearse the narrative like we are practicing for a screenplay, then wonder what happened when the devil moves in for the kill. "But you don't know what they did to me"! My response to this is "You apparently don't know what Jesus did FOR you". For your ease of getting over it before you get devoured, I have added a form just for you to use as needed!

BUTT HURT REPORT FORM

Date of this report:_____ Whiner's name:_____

Name of person perpetrating the butt hurt:_____

Date feelings were hurt:_____ Time of hurtfulness:_____

Location of hurtful incident:_____

Church members sympathetic to whiner:_____

How was hurtfulness communicated? Oral____ Written____ Both____

Is there permanent damage to your feelings? _____ Did you require a tissue? _____

Did you lose sleep? _____ Do you require inner healing? _____

Did you develop Carpal Tunnel from typing up lengthy, butt-hurt rebuttals? _____

Reason for filing this report (mark all that apply)

_____I am thin-skinned _____My feelings are easily hurt _____They looked at me wrong

_____I'm sure they talked about me behind my back _____ They ignored me/didn't shake my hand _____ They didn't immediately respond to my text message

_____Their intent was obvious from what I overheard

_____ They didn't agree with my social media post

_____ They are obviously entertaining demons that no one else sees

Have you taken any action toward the perpetrator of the butt-hurt? If so, what did you do? Please disclose the names of everyone you told your side to, with their response. _____

_____

Describe in your own words why your itty, bitty feelers were hurt: _____

_____

_____

Name of whiner (Printed)_____ Signature of whiner_____
.

This form is not intended to be callous, but to help you see what this really looks like in the shadow of the cross. Forgiveness is critical to alignment, and alignment is critical for survival!

ALIGNMENT

> *"And He gave some as apostles, and some as prophets, and some as evangelists, and some as pastors and teachers, for the equipping of the saints for the work of service, to the building up of the body of Christ; until we all attain to the unity of the faith, and of the knowledge of the Son of God, to a mature man, to the measure of the stature which belongs to the fullness of Christ"* (Eph 4:11-13, NASB 1995).

In Paul's letter to the Ephesians, we read of what's commonly called the five-fold ministry offices. Most of my ministry school students attempt to identify as one of these until they study the rest of the passage! Who are these ministers, and what is their responsibility? Jesus made it very clear that we are ALL called to do the work of the ministry. (All means everyone, by the way.) Unfortunately, that interpretation has been largely lost through history or downplayed in many churches. PLUS, most church goers haven't been equipped, are afraid to ask what it would look like, and don't really want to step out in faith at that level.

What does it mean to be "equipped"? The Greek word for equipping is katartizó (G2675), which means to mend, perfectly join together, repair, or adjust. Luke 6:40 (BSB) says, *"A disciple is not above his teacher, but everyone who is fully trained will be like his teacher".* Fully trained is katartizó, mended, adjusted, aligned. The FIRST thing that happens in Eph 4 is alignment, mending, adjusting. Without alignment, the rest doesn't happen.

What is the rest? Building up of the body of Messiah, unity of the faith, knowledge of the Son of God, maturity, and fullness. Building up is the word for an architectural structure. This is the backbone of the faith. The steel girders that hold everything in place. Unity here is oneness, echad (which we will discuss further on). Knowledge of the Son is a personal, experiential knowing, NOT simply knowing about Him, but truly knowing Him. Note that maturity and fullness are mentioned last. That's because true maturity cannot happen without alignment, without structure, without oneness, and without personally, deeply knowing HIM. "The body of Christ is immature because it is out of alignment" (Nash, 2024, p. 11).

Many years ago, the Lord sent me to a small, local church because the pastor cried out to Him for true revival. Not just a brief, emotional gathering or a guest evangelist preaching a few nights, but a genuine, powerful outpouring of God's Spirit—like the Azusa Street revival, Brownsville, or other historic moves of God that change lives and shift entire communities.

This was to be our third assignment in pursuit of that divine outpouring. In the past, issues had cropped up in the churches we served—conflicts and spiritual barriers that leadership was either unable or unwilling to confront. As a result, the Holy Spirit's move was hindered, and we had to move on, trusting that God would lead us to where He wanted to work.

But this time, I believed, things would be different. This time, God's Spirit would break through. There would be a true outpouring—a fresh wave of His power that would transform hearts, renew lives, and impact the surrounding community in ways that only Heaven could orchestrate.

I pulled out all the stops- next level fasting and prayer, seeking (actually begging) God to give us a major outpouring. I never stopped to consider how a small church would handle large crowds. Red flags began popping up. I ignored them. As the old war saying goes, full speed ahead and damn the torpedoes!

I believed everyone else wanted the same thing. They didn't. I believed that when the power came, Holy Spirit would cover the details. Most importantly, I believed I was covered, that I had an apostolic covering, a pastoral covering, and my husband on board. I could not have been more wrong! I took on regional principalities to clear the atmosphere. The men in my life ran for cover. I didn't see it, so I pressed on.

What I didn't realize was that this congregation REALLY wanted business as usual with some healings and miracles, and some warm fuzzies thrown in for good measure. NO ONE was willing to pay the price. No one was willing to let Holy Spirit strip them of their junk and baggage. Deep surrender? Radical humility? Repentance? That was too much.

What I discovered was devastating. Behind my back, people were speaking evil of me. The enemy worked overtime, trying to stop any work of the Spirit from moving forward. Because there were so many open doors allowing lies, gossip, and division, the enemy had a field day. It was as if the enemy had free rein. Eventually, I received what's called the "left foot of fellowship"—excommunication, separation, rejection—WITHOUT EXCEPTION, from people I once considered my closest friends. They turned against me or simply disappeared from my life.

I was utterly broken. I had poured years of my life into these people, investing everything I had, only to feel like it was all for nothing. I wept before the Lord, overwhelmed by grief and confusion.

And then, the Lord's gentle voice came, soothing but piercing:

> "You are out of alignment. When your back is out of alignment, your whole body is crippled with pain, and you can barely move. That is what happened."

I hadn't seen it then. I hadn't realized that the entire body of believers I served—myself included—was out of divine alignment. Our structural supports—our unity, maturity, and spiritual health—were broken down. We were walking in disunity, immaturity, and chaos. The sheer weight of His glory, the fullness of His Presence, would have destroyed us because we weren't prepared.

It wasn't that I wanted something evil—for my heart was truly for God's kingdom. But I was out of sync with the congregation I served and, most critically, out of step with the timing of Holy Spirit. A spirit of *Strong Delusion* had entered, and with it, the *Scatterer*—the one who comes to divide, to disorient, and to break apart. The perpetrator of church splits and divorce.

I sensed something was wrong, but I couldn't quite put my finger on it—until it was too late.

THE SPIRIT OF DELUSION

How do we get attacked by a spirit of delusion? *We want something so badly that the thing we want, even if it seems Godly, becomes an idol!*

Idolatry is associated with a strong delusion.

> *Jer 10:15: They (idols) are worthless and devoid of promise, a work of delusion and mockery; In their time of [trial and] punishment, they will perish [without hope] (AMP).*

Creating an idol brings a worthless delusion. The very thing WE believe is a promise, even from God, mocks us in the time of our greatest trial. The promise, instead of being a joy and delight, and an answer to prayer, brings death.

The immediate aftermath of stepping into a powerful delusion is believing a lie.

> 2 Thes 2:10-11: "because they refused the love of the truth that would have saved them. For this reason God will send them a powerful delusion so that they believe the lie" (BSB).

Why? It's easier than we think to believe a lie, especially if the LOVE of the truth isn't in us. The Greek word for love here is "agapeo"—not just a casual belief, but a deep, unconditional love for God's Word. This isn't mere acknowledgment; it's an affection that loves His truth regardless of how it feels or what it costs.

This love for His Word means we trust it even when it hurts, believing it as absolute truth and acting upon it. It's resting fully on His promises, but also embracing His correction—being okay when He says, "No." It's loving Him enough to accept His discipline, knowing that His ways are perfect.

The danger of delusion is described by the Greek word "Planos", meaning deception, error, wandering, straying from the straight path, or even roaming like a vagabond or impostor. (Strongs G4108)

The spirit of delusion creates chaos and confusion. It causes wandering in the mind—an internal confusion that can eventually lead us to fall off the straight and narrow path God has set before us.

James 5:20 (BSB) reminds us:

> *"Consider this: Whoever turns a sinner from the error (delusion) of his way will save his soul from death and cover over a multitude of sins."*

Walking in delusion is walking in error! It's missing the perfect mark of God's place of healing, protection, and HIS BEST for you!

Walking in delusion leads to death.

In 1 Thes 2:3, Paul writes:

> *"For our appeal does not come from delusion or impure motives, nor [is it motivated] by deceit [our message is complete, accurate, and based on the truth—it does not change]" (AMP).*

This verse highlights a critical truth: delusion stems from impure motives and deception. It's not just a random error or mistake; it originates when our hearts shift away from pure love and devotion to God. Delusion enters when we begin to idolize—when something or someone becomes *more important* to us than our love for God Himself. It's when we place a false hope, a personal agenda, or a distorted perception above the purity of His truth. When our affections and priorities are misaligned, the enemy can easily lead us astray.

When we allow anything to take the place of God in our hearts, we set ourselves up for deception. Our motives become impure, and our message, our faith, our walk, our understanding, become skewed. We start to believe lies, and the truth becomes distorted in our eyes.

WHAT GIVES TRACTION TO THE DELUSION?

Greek for the word Strong (G1753) is: en-ER-gay-ah, from where we get our English word energy. Energy, working, operation, activity. It is power in action, a momentum that propels something. A strong delusion has energy behind it. It creates its own momentum. Unsanctified desires become our center of focus. Lies and deceit separate us from the truth of God's Word in the situation. Notice I said unsanctified desires, not evil desires! These are desires that seem good, but which are NOT in the Father's perfect will for the time and place we are in. They are out of alignment with His will in the moment.

> James 4:3 (BSB) says, "And when you do ask, you do not receive, because you ask with wrong motives, that you may squander it on your pleasures".

What kinds of pleasures are we talking about? It might be to make a name for ourselves or our ministry. It might be to push our ministry agenda. There might be a strong desire for a particular relationship with someone we are enamored with or someone of influence. It may seem very good, but if it's out of alignment with God's intent and purposes, it will break us!

What happens when our backs are out of alignment? We are in pain! We are unable to carry the load we are assigned. We can't carry our weight. Everyone around us suffers. When one member hurts, we all hurt!

Delusions come from denying the truth, not having an unconditional love for God's Word and promise for us, and desiring to believe a lie more than a desire to know His truth in a situation. Impure motives are involved in delusions.

Delusions are stupid! Not my words- God's Word:

> Ecc 7:25 (ISV). *"I committed myself to understand, to learn, to search for wisdom and explanations, and to understand both the evil that is foolishness and the **stupidity** that is delusion".*

One **Hebrew word** for delusion is tormah': Deceit, fraud. It is used to describe actions that are intentionally misleading or dishonest. The devil is INTENTIONALLY dishonest and misleading so he can destroy us! He can SMELL the open door to idolatry and rushes in to capitalize on it before we recognize what he's up to!

DELUSION AND THE SCATTERER

Another Heb word: mad-doo'-akh from na-dach' meaning Scattering, dispersal, seduction. To seduce, entice or draw away. A strong delusion will **seduce us** away from the truth and **scatter us** from God's purpose and plan. The spirit of delusion and the scatterer work together for our destruction!

THE DANGERS OF PROPHECY

There is a subtle yet dangerous temptation for prophets—and anyone bearing a prophetic word—to speak what the people WANT to hear, rather than what God is truly saying. When this happens, a platform is built, followers are gained, and influence is secured. But ultimately, the truth becomes painfully obvious, and the consequences are severe.

When people choose to believe a lie, they are setting themselves up to be seduced away from God, scattered in confusion and deception. They are headed toward judgment, not because God desires to condemn, but because His love is so great that He cannot allow His children to remain in delusion. To do so would be to leave them in the enemy's trap.

Jeremiah 14:14 starkly reminds us:

> *"The prophets are prophesying lies in My name,"*
> *replied the LORD. "I did not send them or appoint*

them or speak to them. They are prophesying to you a false vision, a worthless divination, the futility and delusion of their own minds" (BSB).

This verse reveals that false prophecy is rooted in personal agendas, deception, and a departure from God's true voice. It is a form of futility—empty words spoken out of selfish motives, not divine authority.

People believe what they want to believe!

Is 30:10: *"They say to the seers, 'Stop seeing visions!' and to the prophets, 'Do not prophesy to us the truth! Speak to us pleasant words; prophesy illusions'"* (delusions, deceit) (BSB).

When the spirit of strong delusion rears its ugly head, we must take a step back and examine **the motives of our hearts.** Ask Holy Spirit to reveal anything in our lives that has become an idol, and drop it like it's hot, because it is!

NEVER FORGET: The enemy is out to destroy you and those you love! Don't do life by yourself, and don't leave your loved ones to bleed out!

NEVER FORGET: *"For our struggle is not against flesh and blood, but against the rulers, against the authorities, against the powers of this world's darkness, and against the spiritual forces of evil in the heavenly realms"* (Eph 6:12, BSB). Let me repeat this: Our struggle is NOT against flesh and blood!!!

Until we become one as the Father and His Son, Yeshua, are one, until we walk in true alignment with one another, until we forgive, we will never reach the maturity He desires for us. We need the structural support that comes from proper alignment!

THE PROCRASTINATION STATION

And the winner of the quarterly procrastination award is…drum roll…..

Let's face it. We've all been there. It seems there is always that one team member who waits until the very last minute to jump on board. Last Minute Louis is usually very enthusiastic about the new project. He shares that his part is a done deal.

Then comes the passage of time. Where is Louis? WHERE IS HIS WORK!?! Then, like clockwork, Louis appears—out of breath, papers flying in every direction, with a sheepish "Sorry I'm late." He's got a laundry list of excuses, some old, some freshly invented.

His twin brother, Good Enough Gordon, often shows up just in time to help pick up the pieces. Louis claims that he would be better organized, but Gordon came by and "helped" just before the deadline, so… there's that.

When asked how much he had done before Gordon's arrival, Louis admits, "Not much". Sigh.... Louis and Gordon have done it again. Now, the project's either delayed or rushed and subpar.

Like the loving believer in Jesus that you are, you rip Louis a new one, chew him up and spit him out, leaving him feeling like the pile of dog poo he had to clean up before he came. After all, you self-righteously tell yourself, he had it coming. This was long overdue! The team was left hanging, and it's all his fault. Or is it?

The senior pastor calls you into his office. You've been on staff for a year, and you genuinely love what you do. Now, he shares an exciting vision—a new project the Lord has placed on his heart that could have a major impact on the community. His words thrill you: He wants YOU to be the team lead!

Wow! The weight of such responsibility feels exhilarating. You feel on top of the world, honored that the senior pastor trusts you with this vital venture. It's a moment of divine affirmation.

He begins to outline the team you'll need:

- A detail-oriented person to manage the minutiae.
- A networker to connect with key community leaders.
- A gifted marketer to give the project pizazz.
- A tech person to handle all technical aspects.

You already have your team in mind. But then, the unexpected happens. The pastor says, "Oh, by the way, the lead tech guy, John, just had surgery yesterday and will be out of commission for the next 6-8 weeks." The deadline is tight—just 8 weeks - and it must be completed by core church members.

Your heart drops from the mountaintop to the valley floor. And the challenge deepens. The second tech guy? Peter. He's the very definition of procrastination. His track record is riddled with missed deadlines, even when he's given extra time. You've had more than enough gray hairs from working with him before. John, who always makes sure someone is in the tech booth with Peter "just in case," is now unavailable. Now, the pressure is mounting. The clock is ticking, and the team you envisioned is suddenly short-handed.

The other tech guy is Weird Harold. He got his name from the "BC" days. He met Yeshua a couple of years ago and has come a long way in his faith. He's really nice, willing to do most anything you ask, and is always on time. Harold has some awesome, crazy tech skills!

Harold does, however, have a quirk that he has struggled to overcome. Interventions have been done to no avail. Harold has an aversion to soap and water. No one enjoys being in the same room with him before his monthly bath. Harold's monthly bath day is marked on everyone's calendar because he hugs EVERYONE anywhere near him! Plus, Peter and Harold refuse to work together for obvious reasons.

What to do? Ask Peter and chew your nails to the quick for the next 8 weeks? Ask Weird Harold and remind everyone else to rub Vicks VapoRub under their noses? Sigh...

Is compromise the sole answer to dealing with the procrastinator? What makes the procrastinator tick? Most of them give a variety of excuses for their tardiness. "I work better under pressure". "I had to work overtime a lot this month". "The car (or other needed item) keeps breaking down". "Time got away from me on this project". Can you see the eye rolling going on? Same person...same excuses...every time!

Those of us who dislike confrontation tend to enable the procrastinator. Say what?!? Why would we do that? Well...because we don't like confrontation! What to do? In our storyline, John solved the problem of Peter's procrastination by making sure someone else was scheduled to be present "just in case". This makes Peter feel valued by keeping him on the tech team while enabling his status as the Prince of Procrastination, since there are no real consequences for his tardiness.

As we've all heard, the definition of insanity is doing the same thing over and over, expecting a different result. John's non-solution has now fallen into your capable hands.

It's time to have a heart-to-heart talk with Peter. "Hey, Pete! How's it going"? Peter gives you the eye like "What's this about? Am I in trouble?" You see, Peter knows how everyone in leadership feels about his "gift" of procrastination. He's been waiting for months to be dropped from the tech team. He finally realized that John is comfortable with how things are and is unwilling to rock the boat. He's heard about the big project and also about John's surgery. He's nervously fidgeting with the pen in his hand, waiting for the shoe to drop. What you say next could determine the future of this all-important project, and even Peter's future in his walk with the Lord!

Instead of the expected lecture, you take a different approach. You ask Peter what he's passionate about. Remember the part about identity? If you discover your passion, you will find your calling and can then be positioned into your fit.

In the course of your discussion with Peter, you find out that he spends late nights playing around with graphic design. He's bored with routine tech, but he loves developing flyers, posters, and promo materials. At his day job, he's been presenting his ideas to his boss, who became very excited to try some of Peter's designs. As a result of this new direction, his boss was able to land a big contract, and Peter is currently taking courses in graphic design and marketing in addition to working full-time to support his family.

You also discover that Peter's wife is pregnant with their second child, and while he's excited about the baby, he's also anxious to be a good provider for his family. He's been burning the midnight oil the past two months to finish classes, get his associate's degree, and land the promised promotion before the baby arrives.

Peter, who rarely verbalizes more than a sentence or two, suddenly opens up, and the dam breaks. He apologizes for being late so much and calling in absent at times for his tech shift. He loves Yeshua with all his heart, but with so much on his plate right now, he truly doesn't know what to do! He says he understands if the senior pastor wants him to step down. Peter, who is usually the picture of the typical unemotional male, dissolves into tears.

After he composes himself, you ask him about upcoming assignments for his classes, what's due in the next 6-8 weeks, and what progress he has made. In typical procrastination fashion, he outlines his project but admits he's barely gotten started with it. He just feels so overwhelmed!

You then inquire if he would like to do something very special for Jesus that he is very passionate about. The incredulous look on his face is unmistakable. "Who, me"? You explain the need for the marketing component of the church project and ask how this could be a fit for both his coursework as well as the needs of the church.

Suddenly, Peter becomes animated with ideas! He's already formulating in his mind how all this fits together. Then he looks at you sideways, "What about Sunday morning tech"? You explain that he doesn't have to do that anymore. A replacement will be found. You outline a plan with detailed steps where Peter will have to routinely meet with you and a couple of other people to discuss the progress he's made. You link him to the individual you originally had in mind to head up the marketing portion.

Problem solved? Or is it? Remember, Peter has been the *Prince of Procrastination* for a long time—old habits die hard. You realize that simply scheduling him and setting deadlines isn't enough. To truly move forward, the head of marketing must stay on top of things, giving Peter specific tasks, clear deadlines, and, most importantly, ongoing encouragement and recognition.

Where the rubber meets the road, Peter lights up when he's praised for his work. That's a vital clue. You've learned that acknowledgment fuels his motivation. So, it's essential that the marketing director understands what truly motivates Peter—and that praise and affirmation are powerful tools to keep him engaged and productive.

This approach isn't about micromanaging; it's about strategic leadership. By understanding Peter's motivators, you can help him break free from his old procrastination habits, one small victory at a time. Celebrate progress, no matter how minor, and remind him of the value he brings to the team.

One problem solved. Now, onto Weird Harold. Harold's monthly bath was three days ago, so it's still safe to be around him. You sit down with Harold to have a talk. Harold is also eyeing you with suspicion. The church has "gifted" Harold with enough bath products to supply the entire homeless encampment just outside of town for the next four months. As a matter of fact, unknown to these well-meaning church members, that is where most of these gifts have gone.

You begin, "Harold, have you heard of the exciting new project we are getting ready to launch"? When Harold realizes this latest discussion is not about personal hygiene, he visibly relaxes. "We need someone to lead the tech portion and are wondering if you would be interested."

As you describe the pastor's vision and what the project entails, Harold becomes excited. He, too, is filled with great ideas. He says he is sorry about John's sudden surgery and will pray for his healing, but also states that he's been waiting for a chance to do something like this. Great! You then ask Harold if you can pray for him to have wisdom and insight, and to be a great fit for this team. Harold agrees.

Your prayer goes something like this: "Father God, this is a very important project for this church, but more importantly, it's a very important project for the people of this community and for Harold and the other team members. Grant to Harold an abundance of wisdom for every part of the project that he is involved with. Surround him with favor as with a shield with all the team members (Ps 5:12). As this project wears on, help the team to focus on the tremendous gifts and talents that Harold brings and not his need for personal hygiene as we perceive it. Father, bring healing to Harold's body that he is a sweet fragrance to not only you, but to all of us as well, in Jesus' name we pray. Amen.

You look at Harold to gauge his reaction. Harold looks at you and asks, "Is my body odor really that bad? I thought everyone was just making fun of me. I thought it was a joke". You reply: It gets pretty bad.

Do you feel comfortable telling me your story? Harold then opens up, sharing his story, his voice trembling with emotion. He grew up dirt poor, with parents addicted to drugs. They often couldn't pay the light bill, let alone provide toiletries or warm water for bathing. Harold would sneak over to a friend's house just to take a bath, knowing it was the only way to feel clean and have some dignity at school. But when his father found out, he beat Harold almost to death, telling him, "Don't ever embarrass the family like that again." Harold lifts his shirt to reveal the scars crisscrossing his back— silent reminders of that traumatic past.

He shares, softly, that his parents were killed several years ago in a drug deal gone wrong. The pain is still fresh, still raw. You gently take Harold's hand, looking into his eyes. "Harold, you're safe now. They can't hurt you anymore." He nods, understanding, but you notice the trembling. The memories flood in like a storm— overwhelming, relentless.

You ask softly, "Harold, do you want to be free of this torment? Do you want to find healing?" He hesitates, then whispers, "Of course."

Without hesitation, you call the inner healing team. They are eager and ready to meet with Harold, to guide him on the road to recovery, helping him find healing and wholeness in Messiah.

I realize that these scenarios paint a happily ever after picture and that real life is often far messier and complicated. The point in both of these stories is that teams and churches are for and about people, not projects. Projects are the vehicle that propels the team into a working relationship with each other. They are the means to discover individual talents, strengths, and weaknesses. Projects in the world are about getting things done at the expense of individual people. Projects in the church should be focused on loving and equipping people to shine for the King.

Jesus picked a rag-tag group of young people with which to turn the world upside down. 1 Cor 1:26-29 (BSB) says:

> "Brothers, consider the time of your calling: Not many of you were wise by human standards; not many were powerful; not many were of noble birth. But God chose the foolish things of the world to shame the wise; God chose the weak things of the world to shame the strong. He chose the lowly and despised things of the

world, and the things that are not, to nullify the things that are, so that no one may boast in His presence".

Hear the heart of God in this: NO ONE is perfect. NO ONE hits the mark every time. Team Yeshua is first and foremost about the people, not the project. It's about how we can love each other in our brokenness and spur one another on to great things.

Every team has its dysfunction, its procrastinator, its perfectionist, its Good Enough Gordons. Nowhere in God's word does it say our work must be perfect. It does say in multiple places to love one another.

Before you shoot the messenger, let me define "perfect". Matt 5:48 (NASB, 1995) says, *"Therefore you are to be perfect, as your heavenly Father is perfect".* This verse has a "therefore" in it, so the context preceding the verse is important to its understanding. Jesus is speaking in Matt 5 about what true love looks like. The word "perfect" means to be mature in mental or moral character (G5046).

The context:

> *Matt 5:43-47 "You have heard that it was said, 'Love your neighbor and hate your enemy.' But I tell you, love your enemies and pray for those who persecute you, that you may be sons of your Father in heaven. He causes His sun to rise on the evil and the good, and sends rain on the*

righteous and the unrighteous. If you love those who love you, what reward will you get? Do not even tax collectors do the same? And if you greet only your brothers, what are you doing more than others? Do not even Gentiles do the same"?

We are called to be mature in our love. This means rather than chewing out the Prince of Procrastination and giving them the boot from the team, we focus on the needs of others. It means redirecting our focus from the project to the people. *"(Love) bears all things, believes all things, hopes all things, endures all things. Love never fails."* (1 Cor 13:7-8a, BSB).

We are called to do life together. Every member is vitally important! There are no throw-away people. There are those who choose to walk away, those who choose to rebel, those who refuse correction for a season and present us with greater challenges, but we should never throw anyone away who is willing to follow Yeshua. Instead, we pour out more abundant honor on those less seemly members (1 Cor 12:23).

Eventually, Harold will take more baths!

THE BUILDING STORM

We're a team. We're learning to love. We've committed to doing life together. What could possibly go wrong?

Now Joshua sent men from Jericho to Ai, which is near Beth-aven, east of Bethel, and said to them, "Go up and spy out the land." So the men went up and spied out Ai. They returned to Joshua and said to him, "Do not let all the people go up; only about two or three thousand men need go up to Ai; do not make all the people toil up there, for they are few." So about three thousand men from the people went up there, but they fled from the men of Ai. The men of Ai struck down about thirty-six of their men, and pursued them from the gate as far as Shebarim and struck them down on the descent, so the hearts of the people melted and became as water.

Then Joshua tore his clothes and fell to the earth on his face before the ark of the LORD until the evening, both he and the elders of Israel; and they put dust on their heads. Joshua said, "Alas, O Lord GOD, why did You ever bring this people over the Jordan, only to deliver us into the hand of the Amorites, to destroy us? If only we had been willing to dwell beyond the Jordan! "O Lord, what can I say since Israel has turned their back before their enemies? "For the Canaanites and all the inhabitants of the land will hear of it, and they will surround us and cut off our name from the earth. And what will You do for Your great name?"

So the LORD said to Joshua, "Rise up! Why is it that you have fallen on your face? "Israel has sinned, and they have also transgressed My covenant which I commanded them. (Josh 7:2-11, NASB 1995)

Picture this: Achan's eyes catch sight of the riches—the spoils—lying in wait in Jericho. He whispers to himself, "What harm could this do? No one will miss a few things. The city is being destroyed anyway. I'll just take a little, just a few items."

What Achan didn't see was the tiny, insidious voice— demon whispers urging him to justify his disobedience. He also failed to see the open door, the legal right he was giving the adversary to wreak havoc in the camp of Israel.

But what else did Achan forget? He was part of a team— part of a community under God's covenant. He couldn't have taken Jericho on his own. He was commanded to march around the city with everyone else for seven days, to shout only on the seventh day, and then to go straight up over the crumbled walls. He was to fight shoulder to shoulder with his brothers, perhaps even fight among those who had fallen at Ai.

Most importantly, Achan forgot one fundamental truth: **Adonai Elohim is a HOLY God.**

His sin didn't just affect him; it threatened the entire nation. It opened a door for the enemy to move in where there should have been divine protection.

THE URIM AND THE THUMMIM

Ex 28:15;29-30: *"You shall make a breastpiece of judgment, the work of a skillful workman". "Aaron shall carry the names of the sons of Israel in the breastpiece of judgment over his heart when he enters the holy place, for a memorial before the LORD continually. "You shall put in the breastpiece of judgment the Urim and the Thummim, and they shall be over Aaron's heart when he goes in before the LORD; and Aaron shall carry the judgment of the sons of Israel over his heart before the LORD continually"* (NASB 1995)

What kind of judgment is this?

Why were the Urim and Thummim so important?

> *"He (Joshua) shall stand before Eleazar the priest, who will seek counsel for him before the LORD by the judgment of the Urim. At his command, he and all the Israelites with him—the entire congregation—will go out and come in"* (Num 27:21, BSB).

Urim (Strong, H224) is from a Hebrew root word meaning light or fire. Thummim (Strong, H8550) is from a Hebrew root word meaning complete truth, integrity, and innocence. These items were specifically placed in the breastpiece of JUDGMENT! Moses was instructed by God Himself in its need, plus Moses gave very specific instructions to Joshua regarding their use.

God is light- He illuminates everything around Him. He is also fire, and fire burns! If we are to stand innocent and blameless before God, we must be complete in His righteousness, His Holiness. The enemy is a legalist. Achan violated the legal terms set by God for the removal of Jericho. Satan stood before God to accuse Achan of his crimes. Because there was no blood covering, men died.

Where did Joshua go wrong? First, he listened to the council of men: *"There is no need to send all the people; two or three thousand men are enough to go up and attack Ai. Since the people of Ai are so few, you need not wear out all our people there"* (Josh 7:3, BSB). According to Moses' specific instructions, he was to consult with Eleazar, who was to seek the counsel of the Lord. If Joshua had done THAT, the sin of Achan would have been pointed out and dealt with before the loss of 36 innocent lives.

Everyone's part is critical to the mission! A little self-ishness here, a little lie there, sprinkled with a dose of rebellion, and the mission falls apart. In all likelihood, if Achan hadn't disobeyed God, his name would never have been recorded in scripture. He would have been rewarded in heaven for a job well done instead of dying a premature death and being made famous for his sin.

PAUL EN ROUTE TO ROME: HEEDING DIVINE GUIDANCE IN THE STORM

In Acts 27, we find Paul's journey to Rome—an adventure filled with peril and divine intervention. The ship was anchored in a small port in Crete, preparing to sail before the winter storms set in. The pilot and ship's owner, eager to reach a more suitable port, decided to set sail.

But Paul, with divine insight, warned them: *"Men, I can see that our voyage will be filled with disaster and great loss, not only to ship and cargo, but to our own lives as well"* (Acts 27:10, BSB). His warning was ignored.

Soon, a violent storm arose—a tempest so fierce that they had to throw cargo and tackle overboard to lighten the load. Ships don't steer without tackle, yet they abandoned vital equipment in desperation. After fourteen days of battling the storm, they ran aground on a sandbar.

According to a new word from the Lord through Paul, the ship and cargo were lost, but all lives were spared. Those who were in charge of the ship didn't listen to the one man who had the inside track with God and were subsequently left shipwrecked in the storm.

In this situation, Paul was a prisoner, the least of these with no seafaring experience, but his input was vital. Without it, lives would have been lost! If they had heeded Paul's warning, the ship and cargo would have survived.

Storms happen. The fight at Ai was going to happen. The storm that shipwrecked Paul was going to happen. We all face storms in life. John 16:33 (BSB) says: *"I have told you these things so that in Me you may have peace. In the world, you will have tribulation. But take courage; I have overcome the world!"*

THE KING OF KINGS. THE STORM OF STORMS.

The year was 30 AD—an unforgettable, monumental year in the history of Israel and the world. Yeshua, the most controversial figure to ever walk the land, had been performing astonishing healings and miracles— signs and wonders that challenged every religious tradition and authority.

His raising of Lazarus from the dead on the fourth day was unprecedented—something no one had ever witnessed before. The people, overwhelmed with awe and hope, cried out, "Hosanna!"—which means "Save us to the uttermost." Their hearts burned with anticipation, ready to crown Him king and overthrow the oppressive Roman rulers.

But this moment of divine victory was also a turning point. The religious leaders, seeing their authority threatened, faced a stark choice: take a stand against Yeshua or risk losing everything, including their power and influence. The tension in that hour was thick with anticipation, rebellion, and the pounding hope of a nation longing for deliverance.

On Nisan 14—Passover—history reached its divine climax. It was the day the spotless Lamb was sacrificed on Golgotha, a place known as "the place of the skull." According to Jewish tradition, Golgotha is where the head of Goliath, the giant David defeated, was buried (1 Samuel 17:54).

As the Lamb of God was suspended between heaven and earth, at that exact moment, Yeshua of Nazareth—the Messiah, the Son of God—uttered the words, "It is finished." This phrase, in its original meaning, is "paid in full." No longer would there be a need for annual sacrifices; the price for sin had been paid once and for all, forever.

The seed of the woman, promised in Genesis 3:15, had crushed the serpent's head through His sacrifice, sealing victory over sin and death.

John the Baptizer, the prophet and forerunner, declared it plainly from the beginning:

> *"Behold, the Lamb of God who takes away the sin of the world"* (John 1:29, NASB).

The first coming of Yeshua was never about being a world ruler or a conquering king of that age. His coming was a direct fulfillment of the spring feast days, the blood of the sacrificial lamb, conquering sin, death, hell, and the grave.

The storm had begun, both outside and within. The disciples, paralyzed by fear, fled and hid in darkness. The once-bold Simon Peter, overwhelmed by shame and remorse, had denied even knowing Yeshua—not once, but three times. His heart shattered as he realized the enormity of his betrayal. Bitter tears streamed down his face, a silent cry of regret.

Night fell like a thick blanket, unbroken and complete—a darkness that was felt as much as seen. It was a night where hell itself seemed to rejoice, celebrating what appeared to be the end of Jesus' mission. Heaven, however, wept in sorrow, mourning the loss of their Savior and the hopes of a broken world.

For the disciples who had left everything behind— their homes, their security, their very futures—nothing remained but despair. The promises they clung to, the prophecies they believed in, seemed to evaporate into the depths of hopelessness. Darkness seemed to have won.

The 15th of Nisan: While the religious leaders celebrated the beginning of the feast of unleavened bread and their supposed victory over the false messiah that they had crucified, the followers of Yeshua, overwhelmed with grief and disbelief, stared into space. Hidden. Feeling abandoned.

It was the Sabbath, the 16th of Nisan—Saturday, a day of rest and mourning. Nothing had changed. The followers of Yeshua sat in darkness, grief heavy upon their hearts. Torah commanded them not to visit the grave, so they sat in silent sorrow, waiting in the shadows of despair. Their hopes, dreams, and promises seemed shattered beyond repair.

The dawn of Nisan 17, the day of First Fruits, broke with a different rhythm—an earthquake of hope and divine power. The women, early in the morning, went to the tomb to anoint His body with perfumes, as was customary after the Sabbath and feast days. But what they found changed everything. The stone was rolled away, and the tomb was empty.

He was no longer there. Yeshua had risen! The impossible had become reality—the resurrected Lord was alive! Night turned into day. As the morning light spread across the sky, the disciples slowly began to grasp what had happened. The words Yeshua had spoken—about His death and resurrection—began to sink in, though many still refused to believe at first.

But the truth could not be contained. Yeshua was back—alive forevermore! His victory over death was complete, sealing our hope for eternity.

Momentous days were ahead. The baptism in fire on Shavuot (Pentecost). Thousands added to the fledgling church. More healings and miracles, this time through the disciples.

Remember John 16:33 about the trouble in this life? That trouble hit with full force. Stephen is stoned to death. James, the brother of John, is beheaded. The church is scattered. The persecution heats up against this new sect of Judaism. How did they survive the storm? Faith in Messiah, trusting in each other, and praying for boldness to spread the Good News of the Kingdom!

> *"They devoted themselves to the apostles' teaching and to the fellowship, to the breaking of bread and to prayer. A sense of awe came over everyone, and the apostles performed many wonders and signs.*
>
> *All the believers were together and had everything in common. Selling their possessions and*

goods, they shared with anyone who was in need.

With one accord, they continued to meet daily in the temple courts and to break bread from house to house, sharing their meals with gladness and sincerity of heart, praising God and enjoying the favor of all the people. And the Lord added to their number daily those who were being saved." (Acts 2:42-47, BSB)

The word "devoted" in verse 42 means "to be earnest towards, to persevere, be constantly diligent" (Strong, G4342).

God has placed within His body many excellent teachers, dedicated apostles, pastors, prophets, and evangelists. Can we say we are *diligent* in studying their teachings? I'm not talking about armchair prophets and keyboard warriors. I'm talking about the true servants of God who have paid a price to pour into the lives of those God has entrusted to them.

Are we earnest toward fellowship, the breaking of bread, and prayer? Do we constantly make excuses why we can't attend a fellowship that God is nudging us toward? "I'm too tired or too busy". "It's too rainy, too cold, too hot outside". "It's too far to drive (30 minutes instead of 15)." "Those people are critical. They will judge me". "I didn't feel any warm fuzzies last time I was in church".

I'm pretty sure Paul and Silas weren't feeling warm fuzzies after being beaten, placed in stocks, and locked in prison, especially after going to Macedonia based on a vision from God (Acts 16). Paul and Silas were building the Kingdom of God for HIS glory, not worshiping the god of me.

Why do so many modern-day believers in Yeshua fall by the wayside? How is it that so many face illness, poverty, and death alone? According to the Pew Research Center (2021), 51% of Protestant Christians attend church, and only 35% of Catholics attend church at least once a month. With 63% of Americans identifying themselves as Christians, that leaves MILLIONS of believers unchurched, without fellowship, without support, and alone in a jacked-up demonized world! How long do you think the first-century church would have survived if they had the same mentality and attendance philosophy that we exhibit today?

> *"Two are better than one, because they have a good return for their labor. For if one falls down, his companion can lift him up; but pity the one who falls without another to help him up! Again, if two lie down together, they will keep warm; but how can one keep warm alone? And though one may be overpowered, two can resist. Moreover, a cord of three strands is not quickly broken"* *(Ecc 4:9-12, BSB).*

How do we face the storms of life? TOGETHER!

PULLING ON STRENGTHS AND COVERING WEAKNESSES

"The body is a unit, though it is composed of many parts. And although its parts are many, they all form one body. So it is with Christ. For in one Spirit we were all baptized into one body, whether Jews or Greeks, slave or free, and we were all given one Spirit to drink.

For the body does not consist of one part, but of many. If the foot should say, "Because I am not a hand, I do not belong to the body," that would not make it any less a part of the body. And if the ear should say, "Because I am not an eye, I do not belong to the body," that would not make it any less a part of the body. If the whole body were an eye, where would the sense of hearing be? If the whole body were an ear, where would the sense of smell be?

But in fact, God has arranged the members of the body, every one of them, according to His design. If they were all one part, where would the body be? As it is, there are many parts, but one body.

The eye cannot say to the hand, "I do not need you." Nor can the head say to the feet, "I do not need you." On the contrary, the parts of the body that seem to be weaker are indispensable, and the parts we consider less honorable, we treat with greater honor. And our unpresentable parts are treated with special modesty, whereas our presentable parts have no such need.

But God has composed the body and has given greater honor to the parts that lacked it, so that there should be no division in the body, but that its members should have mutual concern for one another. If one part suffers, every part suffers with it; if one part is honored, every part rejoices with it".
(1 Cor 12:12-26, BSB)

Psalm 139:14 reminds us, *"I praise you because I am fearfully and wonderfully made."* Truly, every organ, every cell, and every tiny part of our body fulfills a vital purpose. Without the heart, blood stops flowing, and life ends. Without the lungs, oxygen can't reach our cells, and we suffocate. Without the humble organs— the bowels and the rectum—waste wouldn't be eliminated, water wouldn't be recycled, and infection could take hold.

Many parts of our body, when lost or damaged, aren't immediately life-threatening, but life becomes incredibly difficult—if not impossible. Without legs or feet, walking and mobility are hindered; without hands, feeding and grooming become monumental challenges. Lose your vision or hearing, and navigating the world around you becomes next-level hard. Even losing the senses of smell and taste can be dangerous—imagine eating spoiled food without realizing it.

This intricate design highlights how each piece, no matter how small or lowly it may seem, is essential for our survival and well-being. The body's complexity and harmony reflect God's divine wisdom—each part essential, each part precious.

Paul is telling us in 1 Corinthians 12 that there is an important spiritual analogy here. God, Himself, arranged the members of the body according to His design. Who put us where we are? Who arranged us? Who are you, oh man, to tell God he doesn't know what he's doing! Who created whom? Again...He is God, and we are not!

BIBLICAL HONOR

So, what do we do with the "less honorable" parts? We treat them with greater honor! What is honor?

According to Webster's Dictionary (1828), honor is "A testimony of esteem; any expression of respect or of high estimation by words or actions; dignified respect".

Biblical honor in Hebrew is Kahvad' (Strong, H3513), meaning "weighty, to be heavy, to be glorified". This is the term used to describe the weighty Glory of God. It is also the word used in the commandment to "honor" our father and mother. According to my Hebrew teacher, Chaim BenTorah, "The idea of respect and honor in *kahvad'* comes from the idea of heaping praise, respect, and honor on someone, weighing them down with respect". Let that sink in for a moment. God takes honor VERY SERIOUSLY!

To respect someone is to treat them with high regard, or to esteem (Webster, 1828).

Biblical honor in Greek is timaó, meaning "to prize, fix a valuation upon; by implication, to revere -- honor, value".

What does this look like for us today? Sometimes it's striking up a conversation with the person who always sits in the back of the church. It can be as simple as scanning the crowd at the end of an event or service, looking for someone who appears downcast or distraught. It can mean taking a few seconds to ask the Lord to highlight someone and give them a word of knowledge or encouragement. It could mean inviting a newcomer to lunch, and yes, paying for their meal. Remember, you're on kingdom business, and God promises to reimburse your obedience; He will reward your faithfulness.

What happens to the big annual church conference (you know the one where people are radically transformed, saved, and healed by the power of God) when the janitor quits, or the nursery staff doesn't show up? What happens if the toilets back up or the toilet paper runs out, and everyone says, "That's not my job"? What about if the tech guy is having a bad day and shows up 15 minutes after service starts?

If you are on staff when these things go down, what's your response? Do you chew these volunteers up one side and down the other? If so, not only are you dishonoring those less seemly members, but in all likelihood, they will quit, and you will never see them again. Instead of raising up disciples to step into the fullness of their calling, you've just added to the 49% of the unchurched fringe, exposing their flank to the nearest demon.

What to do? You can't cover everything at once. So, you unstop the toilet yourself, you find the key to the paper dispensers, then you see what and who is available to you. I'm not allowed in the tech booth (Apparently, all the buttons look alike to me, and it becomes a comedy of errors!), so I will find someone I know who can fill in. The same for the nursery. First, plug the holes so everything can run as smoothly as possible. THEN address the personnel issues.

Remember Peter and Harold from our earlier story? How about calling or approaching these with love and honor? Find out what happened first. See what can be done to heal the problems, not make them worse. Don't forget, we need EVERYONE to do their part!

One of the biggest mistakes many churches make is overusing and sometimes abusing their volunteers. When someone senses God's call on their life, the instinct might be to place them immediately into roles like nursery or janitorial work, simply filling the gaps. We often see every open spot as a need to be filled, and so we ask faithful believers to serve wherever there's an empty space. Can anyone say: "free slave labor"?

Let's be honest: this approach can lead to burnout, frustration, and even discouragement among those who are faithful. Instead, how about this? We hire people to do the jobs no one wants—positions that require skill and professionalism. Then, we pray and seek God for Him to place in others a heart to step into these roles, or even into new areas of leadership.

Remember, every servant of God who truly makes a difference often started out in humble places—cleaning toilets, taking out trash, or doing menial tasks. That opportunity isn't wrong; it's part of developing humility and character. But, we should never keep faithful servants stuck in those roles indefinitely, forgetting that God may have a promotion—like He did for Joseph—waiting for them in due time.

TORAH'S TYPES AND SHADOWS

The Covenant under Moses, the Torah, carries much significance for us today if we choose to dig a little. Numbers chapter four contains some interesting types and shadows for the temple service. It begins by taking a census of three different families descended from the tribe of Levi. It then goes on to relate the specific type of service each of the three families is to carry out concerning the temple when it is time to pack up and move. Say what?? What do the details of packing up and moving the tabernacle have to do with honor? Let's look a little deeper.

The first are the sons of K'hat. They were tasked with carrying the especially Holy items, including the Ark! Remember the Ark? This is the very same Ark that, when touched by Uzzah, fried him to a crisp (2 Sam 6:6-7). This is the Ark that was only approached ONCE a year by the high priest, and he had to wear bells on his garment and a rope around his ankle in case he dropped dead in God's presence! The High Priest and his sons were tasked with carefully packing up all these items, and then the sons of K'hat carried them. The name K'hat means allied.

The second family, the sons of Gershon, were tasked with packing up and moving the curtains, tapestries, ropes, etc., of the tabernacle. The name Gershon means a refugee or outcast and comes from the root word garash (Strong, H1644), meaning to drive away, expel, thrust out, or expatriate.

The third family, the sons of M'rari, were tasked with carrying the poles, the framework, the rigid structure of the tabernacle. The name M'rari means bitter, to be moved with grief.

Are you seeing the picture yet? Those you are aligned with, your allies, the faithful ones, are easy to honor with the carrying of that which is Holy to the Lord. These have labored among you, and they can be trusted.

What about the others? What about those who have been outcasts? Are the members of the body who have been kicked to the curb by others important for kingdom purposes? Maybe, like Joseph and David, God is testing them for such a time as this! Every outcast, every wounded soul, holds a vital piece in God's grand design—sometimes the very piece needed to complete His masterpiece.

What about the bitter? What do we do with those who have wept bitter tears and feel as though life has passed them by? These are the ones we heap on more abundant honor! These were tasked with the heavy lifting. These were positioned by God to carry the very framework of His tabernacle!

We in Messiah's body who have been positioned to raise up disciples, must do THAT, not try to constantly fill holes with warm bodies! Love on and heal the brokenhearted. Help them to find their identity and purpose, then position them accordingly, trusting God that He knows what He's doing! When someone makes a mess, clean it up, help them out of the ditch, and start over again. We MUST cease judging and condemning God's kids, Yeshua's bride, because they did something we don't like. Quit worshiping the god of me and learn to love.

When Paul speaks of unpresentable body parts—those that require modesty—we instinctively understand the reference to physical anatomy. But spiritually, how does this relate?

God's original command to Adam and Eve was to be fruitful and multiply. He gave the same divine mandate to the church: to reproduce spiritually by sharing the Good News of the Kingdom. How do we do this? What does it look like in our local body of believers?

Churches MUST reproduce or they will die! A vibrant church births something all the time. God inspired programs, trainings, meetings, outreaches, home groups, etc., that speak to people's needs and bring healing to their hearts are born. New believers are said to be "born again". How does this happen? How do we know what tools God wants us to use to advance His Kingdom? These are birthed in the place of prayer. In the secret place, hidden away from the platforms, the eyes of men, and the social media posts.

This vital, unseen army is the intercessors. These are members of the body that stay hidden, remaining in the background, doing what they are called to do. They give voice to the desires of the King, speaking into existence the things that were not as though they are (Rom 4:17). They war against forces of darkness so that the other members can be who they are called to be, doing what they are called to do.

A CALL TO SENIOR PASTORS

Let me ask you directly: how are you valuing and covering your intercessors? Do you truly appreciate the vital role they play in the health and growth of your church? Or do you dismiss their prophetic words as "crazy" or "over-the-top"?

The truth is, intercessors pour out their hearts and spirits in prayer not for themselves, but for YOU and the church God has entrusted to your care. Are you asking Holy Spirit to give them wisdom and insight? Are you seeking their counsel, or are you dismissing what they carry?

Leadership must understand this: **the most significant spiritual breakthroughs—outpourings of the Holy Spirit—never happen without intercessors.** No great move of God has ever occurred without a dedicated, fervent prayer movement behind it.

THE KEY

At the heart of God's design is unity—an unbreakable bond of love and care among His people. When we truly value each other, respect each other's gifts, and faithfully serve one another, there is no room for division. Instead, there is strength, harmony, and unstoppable progress in His kingdom.

Caring for one another minimizes suffering. When one member of the body falls into the ditch—whether through hardship, mistake, or spiritual attack—many hands are ready to lift them up again. No one is left alone. No one is cast aside.

ECHAD

Echad (Strong, H259) is Hebrew for "one." But it's important to clarify—this isn't simply the number one as represented by the letter aleph. Instead, *echad* signifies a perfect oneness of relationship. It connotes a unity that is profound, complete, and inseparable. This is the same word used to describe the relationship between the Father, the Son, and the Spirit—one God in perfect unity.

In human relationships, *echad* is exemplified when a man and a woman marry; they become "one flesh" (Genesis 2:24). It's a union that transcends mere physical connection, embodying spiritual and relational harmony.

ECHAD VERSUS UNITY

It's crucial to distinguish *echad* from *unity*. The Hebrew word *Chabar* (Strong, H2266) is often translated as "unity" or "to unite." It implies forming an alliance, establishing fellowship, or joining together. Similarly, *Lahav* (Strong, H3867) means "to join," "to cleave," or even "to borrow" or "to lend"—as in a financial obligation. You are united or *lahav* with someone when you borrow money from them until you pay it back.

Psalm 133:1 says: *"Behold, how good and how pleasant it is for brothers to dwell together in unity" (NASB 1995)!* The Hebrew word here for unity is Yachad (Strong, H3162) and means...well... unity. It means to be together.

Webster (1828) defines unity as "a thing undivided itself, but separate from every other thing. Agreement. Unity of faith is an equal belief of the same truths of God, and possession of the grace of faith in like form and degree".

Webster then goes on to define oneness under the definition of unity as follows: "Unity of spirit, is the oneness which subsists between Christ and his saints, by which the same spirit dwells in both, and both have the same disposition and aims" (1828).

Unity is where all members have the same beliefs, but oneness is where the Spirit of God is leading, and we flow together because we are filled with the same Spirit. Unity is a joining together for a common purpose, and can be the process that leads toward being one, but it doesn't have to. When the common purpose has ended, the unity ends unless the members have become one with each other. "Unity builds upon an event. Oneness transcends the event to establish spiritual alignment". (Nash, 2024, p. 81)

I lead a group called *The Wellness Warriors*, a community that meets regularly in my home to share a meal, exchange healthy food ideas, and dive into teaching about nourishing our bodies. We enjoy good food—recipes rooted in health and vitality—and discuss what Jesus might eat if He were living in today's society. Our core values—faith, health, and community—bind us together, regardless of our individual struggles.

Most of us are battling weight issues and food-related illnesses. We all share a common desire: to eat intentionally and healthily, not just to look good, but to be able to run the race Jesus has set before us—with energy, purpose, and strength. We want to serve on the front lines, not from our recliners.

When we come together, we are in unity—a unity of purpose and heart. We share the same values, the same goal: to honor God with our bodies, to support one another, and to become healthier versions of ourselves so we can fulfill His calling on our lives. This is what unity is all about.

Let's say a tragedy strikes one of our members, for example, a family member is in the hospital in critical condition. Suddenly, the values and goals have changed as this group member is stuck eating out of the hospital vending machine, or have they?

If, as a group, we say "You are in our thoughts and prayers", <u>but do nothing else</u>, we are still in unity when we meet as a group, but we are not one, because *echad* goes beyond mere agreement or shared words.

True *echad* is demonstrated when, as a group, we respond to the needs of one of our own in genuine love and action. When we hear the call, we band together, creating a meal train for the family, buying or packing snacks to take to the hospital, or pitching in to handle additional chores, whether it's cleaning a house, caring for pets, or simply providing emotional support.

When we have truly become one body, when one member suffers, we all suffer. When another rejoices, we all rejoice (1 Cor 12:26). Apostle Clay Nash says it best when he wrote: "In unity, people assemble for common interest, but in oneness, people are fitly joined together for kingdom purpose" (2024, p. 89).

We can see where *echad*, oneness, is important in close relationships such as marriage, but what about in the church? Is this level of relationship Biblical? Is it even possible?

Yeshua's final prayer- the one that has yet to be answered:

> *"I am no longer in the world; and yet they themselves are in the world, and I come to You. Holy Father, keep them in Your name, the name*

which You have given Me, that they may be one even as We are.

"I do not ask on behalf of these alone, but for those also who believe in Me through their word; that they may all be one; even as You, Father, are in Me and I in You, that they also may be in Us, so that the world may believe that You sent Me. "The glory which You have given Me I have given to them, that they may be one, just as We are one; I in them and You in Me, that they may be perfected in unity, so that the world may know that You sent Me, and loved them, even as You have loved Me".
(John 17:11; 17:20-23, NASB)

When scripture says "truly, truly, it's like adding an exclamation point to the sentence. Yeshua repeats the phrase "that they may be one, even as we are" (perfected in unity means the same thing) FOUR TIMES! He's not only emphasizing this, He's crying out: THAT THEY MAY BE ONE!!! He's screaming, "Father, do a work in these people you have given me that when they are filled with Holy Spirit, they become ECHAD! Can you hear it? Can you feel His cry?

THE DANGER OF DIVISION AND THE POWER OF AGAPE LOVE

This prayer has yet to be answered. Far too often, we form groups, ministries, small communities, even churches, only to see the enemy whisper his lies and sow seeds of discord. These divisions lead us to blame one another, to harbor hurt feelings, and to withdraw in fear. We seek out others who share our values, our beliefs about the Kingdom, but because of past wounds, we keep them at arm's length.

We rarely stand back-to-back with one another in spiritual battle, defending each other with unwavering loyalty. Instead, we draw back, leaving brothers and sisters bleeding in the midst of the fight. And then, when we face our own crises, we become surprised and angry because no one comes to our rescue. We wonder why the world is reluctant to join us, why they see no real Kingdom purpose.

But Yeshua gave us a clear command:

> "A new commandment I give you: Love one another. As I have loved you, so you also must love one another. By this everyone will know that you are My disciples, if you love one another." (John 13:34-35, BSB)

The word *agapeo* (Strong, G25) describes this love—a selfless, unconditional love that seeks the highest good of others without expectation of return. It's not optional; it's an imperative. This love is at the very heart of Kingdom growth and the salvation of the world.

Yeshua didn't say that the world would recognize His followers by healings, miracles, signs, and wonders alone. While these demonstrations of power may attract attention, they don't sustain or establish a lasting relationship. Instead, what truly binds us as *echad*—as one— is love.

Love is the glue that holds the body together. It's what keeps us unified in purpose, rooted in humility, and committed to one another through thick and thin. Without love, even the most spectacular signs eventually fade, and the unity we think we have begins to fracture.

The world's greatest witness isn't just the power displayed; it's the genuine love that flows between believers—selfless, unconditional, and sacrificial. That love—*agape*—is what demonstrates that we are truly His disciples. It's the tangible evidence that we have become *echad* as Yeshua and the Father are *echad*.

CONCLUSION (But Not Really)

This may be the conclusion of this book, but it is far from the end of the story. When I began writing this for my ministry school students, my goal was to create a handbook grounded in Scripture, something that would help them navigate the many pitfalls and demonic traps constantly arrayed against those doing life together in Messiah. I wanted to provide insight that could serve as a guiding light through the wilderness seasons I have personally walked.

In truth, I realized that the lessons I've learned, the struggles I've endured, and the victories I've celebrated are not meant for me alone. They are for the body of Messiah; for every believer who longs to walk in truth, unity, and purpose.

When I write, I am diligent to research thoroughly, verify sources, and study the original language of Scripture. As much as it depends on me, I seek to ensure that what I share is accurate, relevant, and anointed by the

Spirit. At the foundation of all I do is prayer: "Yeshua, what do You want to say to Your people?"

This book took me places I never thought I'd go. I saw things, felt things, and wept for my King. I saw His heart for us and thought, "Oh God, I must protect your heart at all costs".

He doesn't care if we put together an effective team to accomplish great things for Him. He... doesn't... care. The cry of His heart is that we are ONE, as He and the Father are one. This means that we must be immersed in His Presence, seeing HIS kingdom goals, and follow HIS lead. Together. This is profound in its simplicity. Yet we miss it all the time!

Instead of this being just a book about team participation from a biblical perspective, it has become a blueprint—an answer to Yeshua's final prayer in John 17. As far as I can tell, this prayer is the only one He offered while walking this earth that remains largely unfulfilled. The early church understood this truth far better than we do. Despite their many shortcomings, they turned the world upside down for the King.

We, with nearly two thousand years of history behind us, have the benefit of lessons learned, mistakes corrected, and strategies refined. Yet, despite this, we still stumble, fall, and fail again and again.

Division, disunity, self-righteousness, backbiting, selfishness, and unforgiveness are tools of the enemy that have been used successfully for centuries against mankind. We should know better by now, yet they still work! We know that we wrestle not against flesh and blood but demons, yet flesh and blood are the immediate recipients of our counter-attack. We allow the devil's lies to separate us from the very brothers and sisters who are equipped to defend us, then wonder why the attack was so swift and horrific. In short, we continue to serve the "god of me".

Can we truly run alongside everyone who claims Yeshua as their Messiah? The honest answer is no. The Bible warns us that there will be many with ulterior motives—self-proclaimed prophets, prideful hearts, unrepentant spirits, and those who refuse to be teachable. These individuals do not share our true values, nor are they genuinely interested in walking in truth.

The early church faced the same challenge and warned us about false teachers and wolves in sheep's clothing. How do we recognize them? They are not isolationists; rather, they seek to build followers through manipulation, preying on the unsuspecting and biblically naive. They rarely operate in love. They have no true understanding of biblical love. Instead, they serve the "god of me," expecting others to do the same.

Such individuals attack those who seek to correct them, leaving their followers shipwrecked in their spiritual journey. They sow discord, confusion, and division, all while claiming to represent Yeshua.

Therefore, do NOT associate with these counterfeit believers. They are not part of the true body of Messiah. Their goal is to lead many astray, and their influence is destructive. The Word commands us clearly: *"Flee from such as these!"* (2 Timothy 3:5).

For the rest: Can we learn to love before it's too late? Can we pursue God's will and heart for our lives against all odds? Can we truly become who He intended us to become? Can we quit making converts and leaving them by the roadside to die? Can we cease with the fancy programs and pithy one-liners that serve to tickle men's ears, but don't produce disciples? Can we, like the good Samaritan, bind up even our enemy's wounds? Can we learn what it looks like to be one? Are we willing to answer Yeshua's prayer no matter the cost?

> *"That they may all be one; even as You, Father, are in Me and I in You, that they also may be in Us, so that the world may believe that You sent Me"* (John 17:21, NASB).

The question remains: Will we rise to the challenge? Will we choose love: authentic, sacrificial, divine love, and walk in the unity that Yeshua prayed for? The time to decide is now. The call is clear. The Kingdom awaits.

REFERENCES

BenTorah, Chaim. (2025). *Hebrew Word Study- Honor-Kavod*. Retrieved from the subscription portion.

BenTorah, Chaim. (2024). *Hebrew Word Study- Woman-'Isah*. Retrieved from https://www.chaimbentorah.com/2024/08/hebrew-word-study-woman-isah/

BenTorah, Chaim. (2022). *Aramaic Word Study-Weaker Vessel- Mana Machal*. Retrieved from https://www.chaimbentorah.com/2022/07/aramaic-word-study-weaker-vessel-mana-machal/

BenTorah, Chaim. (2019). *Hebrew Word Study- Handmaiden*. Retrieved from https://www.chaimbentorah.com/2019/09/hebrew-word-study-handmaiden/

BenTorah, Chaim. (2018). *Hebrew Word Study- Feather and Wings*. Retrieved from https://www.chaimbentorah.com/2018/07/hebrew-word-study-feathers-and-wings/

BenTorah, Chaim. (2018). Journey Into Silence. Witaker House. New Kensington, PA.

BenTorah, Chaim. (2016). *Hebrew Word Study: Revealing the Heart of God*. Whitaker House, New Kensington, PA.

Chaudhry R, Usama SM, Babiker HM. *Physiology, Coagulation Pathways*. [Updated 2023 Aug 28]. In: StatPearls [Internet]. Treasure Island (FL): StatPearls Publishing; 2025 Jan. Retrieved from: https://www.ncbi.nlm.nih.gov/books/NBK482253/

Green, D. (2006). *Coagulation Cascade*. PubMed. https://pubmed.ncbi.nlm.nih.gov/17022746/

Mast, Dale L. (2015). *And David Perceived He Was King. Identity- the Key to Your Destiny*. Xulon Press.

Nash, Clay (2024). *Aligned for Conquest*. Clay Nash Ministries.

Pew Research Center. (2021). *About three-in-ten U.S. Adults are now Religiously Unaffiliated*. Retrieved from https://www.pewresearch.org/religion/2021/12/14/about-three-in-ten-u-s-adults-are-now-religiously-unaffiliated/

Stern, David. (2021). *The Complete Jewish Study Bible*. Hendrickson Bibles. Messianic Jewish Publishers.

Strong, James. (n.d.). *Strong's Exhaustive Concordance of the Bible*. In https://biblehub.com/

Webster, Noah. (1828). *Webster's Dictionary*.
In https://webstersdictionary1828.com/

Williams Institute (2023). *How Many Youth and Adults Identify as Transgender in the United States?* UCLA School of Law. Retrieved from https://williamsinstitute. law.ucla.edu/publications/trans-adults-united-states/